RETURN OF THE JEDI

The release of *Star Wars: The Empire Strikes Back* confirmed the lasting appeal of George Lucas's *Star Wars*, expanding and adding depth to the characters while leaving audiences thirsty for more thanks to a dramatic ending that made good on the saga's origins as a cliffhanger serial.

The final episode of the saga (at least at that time), *Return of the Jedi,* was released on May 25, 1983. Tasked with resolving the revelations of its predecessor and bringing the story of Luke Skywalker, Princess Leia, and Han Solo's battle against the Empire to a conclusion, it succeeded in not only wrapping up the story but also delivered some dramatic revelations too.

Through interviews with the cast and crew, production photos, and original concept art, this souvenir special edition delves into the story behind the groundbreaking movie.

TITAN EDITORIAL
Editor Jonathan Wilkins
Writer Chris Cooper
Group Editor Jake Devine
Art Director Oz Browne
Editorial Assistant Ibraheem Kazi
Production Controller Kelly Fenlon
Production Controller Caterina Falqui
Production Manager Jackie Flook
Sales & Circulation Manager
Steve Tothill
Marketing Coordinator Lauren Noding
Publicity & Sales Coordinator
Alexandra Iciek
Publicist Caitlin Storer
Digital & Marketing Manager
Jo Teather
Head of Business & Creative
Development Duncan Baizley
Publishing Directors Ricky Claydon
& John Dziewiatkowski

Executive Vice President
Andrew Sumner
Publishers Vivian Cheung &
Nick Landau

DISTRIBUTION
U.S. Distribution: Penguin
Random House
U.K. Distribution: MacMillian
Distribution
Direct Sales Market: Diamond
Comic Distributors
General Inquires: cutomerservice@
titanpublishingusa.com

First Edition May, 2024
Printed in China

*Star Wars: Return of the Jedi 40th
Anniversary Special Edition* is published
by Titan Magazines, a division of
Titan Publishing Group Limited, 144
Southwark Street, London SE1 0UP
Printed in the China

For sale in the U.S., Canada, U.K.,
and Eire
ISBN: 9781787740792
Titan Authorized User. TMN 13736

No part of this publication may be
reproduced, stored in a retrival system,
or transmitted, in any form or by
any means, without the prior written
permission of the publisher.
A CIP catalogue record for this title is
available from the British Library.

10 9 8 7 6 5 4 3 2 1

LUCASFILM EDITORIAL
Senior Editor Brett Rector
Art Director Troy Alders
Creative Director Michael Siglain
Story Group Leland Chee, Pablo
Hidalgo, Kate Izquierdo
Creative Art Manager Phil Szostak
Asset Management Chris
Argyropoulos, Gabrielle Levenson,
Elinor De La Torre, Michael Trobiani,
Sarah Williams

Special Thanks: Samantha Keane
and Kevin Pearl

CONTENTS

THE MYTH GROWS...

Star Wars: A New Hope hadn't just taken the world by storm in 1977, it had taken it by surprise, forever redefining what audiences could expect from a fantasy adventure movie. It's sequel, *Star Wars: The Empire Strikes Back* (1980), had exceeded all expectations by adding rich new colors to the already vivid palette of the first movie. With the high drama of Darth Vader's "I am your Father!" revelation,

the spiky romance between Han Solo and Princess Leia, the mysticism of Yoda and mystery of Boba Fett, and some of the most thrilling visual effects to ever grace the silver screen, it's safe to say that the third film in the trilogy would have a lot to live up to.

Star Wars: Return of the Jedi was slated for release in 1983, with a mission to resolve the saga in a way that would leave fans, both casual and devoted, feeling just as satisfied and with all their questions answered. Behind the scenes, its success

would be just as important to the futures of Lucasfilm and Industrial Light & Magic, the companies George Lucas had created in order to help him make the kind of movies he was interested in making. The journey from Lucas' famous yellow notepaper to script then pre-production, filming, and eventual release would be as much of a rollercoaster ride as any speeder bike chase through the forests of Endor. This is the story of how the Jedi returned, and the *Star Wars* saga reached its (then) epic conclusion.

The theatrical advance one-sheet, or teaser poster (left), for *Star Wars: Return of the Jedi* illustrated by Drew Struzan.

RETURN OF THE JEDI
By Numbers

6 Puppeteers operating Jabba the Hutt

11 Age of Wicket actor Warwick Davis

22 feet Width of the Death Star II reactor model

88 days Duration of principal photography

131 minutes Running time

820 Theaters on opening

$23,019,618 Opening weekend box office gross

$475,106,177 Worldwide Box Office Gross

A Partial List of Costs

AT-ST walker model head: **$500**

Morrison's Creek (Endor) location fee: **$5,000**

Life-size rancor arm: **$63,923**

Sails for Jabba the Hutt's barge: **$70,000**

Foreground creatures: **$715,724**

Death Star II hangar set: **$750,000**

Principal cast fee: **$1,992,709**

Makeup and Hair: **$2,234,940**

Production insurance: **$4,000,000**

Set construction: **$5,909,976**

Initial budget: **$32,500,000**

Final cost: **$42,675,038**

THE SAGA SO FAR

The runaway success of *Star Wars: A New Hope* in 1977 had given George Lucas confidence to continue his story with 1980's *The Empire Strikes Back.* However, that film had seen its budget balloon, forcing the saga's creator to put his hands in his pockets or face financial ruin in order to get the film completed.
A sizable hit, *The Empire Strikes Back* ended on a dramatic cliffhanger as the depleated rebel forces licked their wounds, Han Solo's fate hung in the balance as he was captured by Boba Fett, and Luke Skywalker was left pondering a devastating truth about his parentage.

ACT ONE:

In which the lead characters and the galaxy they inhabit are established, and the premise of the story is laid out. An inciting event leads the hero on a path of discovery.

STAR WARS: A NEW HOPE

An Imperial Star Destroyer closes in on a much smaller vessel, pounding it's hull with laser canons. White armored stormtroopers board the ship, quickly taking control before their commander—Darth Vader, Dark Lord of the Sith—joins them.

Meanwhile, Princess Leia records a holographic plea for help and entrusts it, along with the stolen plans, to the droid R2-D2. The astromech and his counterpart, C-3PO, jettison from the ship in an escape pod, landing on the desert planet Tatooine. Still onboard, Leia is

captured by Vader's troops and taken to the Death Star, where the Sith Lord subjects her to interrogation.

On Tatooine, the droids are captured by Jawas and sold on to moisture farmer Owen Lars, who tells his nephew, Luke Skywalker, to clean them up. As he does so, Luke trigger's Leia's hidden message: "Help me, Obi-Wan Kenobi. You're my only hope."

That night, R2-D2 sneaks off into the desert to search for Kenobi; and the following morning Luke and C-3PO search for him in the Jundland Wastes and are attacked by sandpeople. They are saved by an old man who reveals himself to be the very Kenobi R2-D2 has been searching for.

Kenobi tells Luke that he was friends with the boy's father and fought alongside him in the Clone Wars. After presenting Luke with his father's lightsaber, Obi-Wan listens to Leia's entire

message, in which she asks for the the former Jedi Knight's help in delivering the Death Star plans to her father on Alderaan. Obi-Wan asks Luke to go with him on his journey and train in the ways of the Force, but the boy is unsure, offering only to take Kenobi as far as Anchorhead.

On the way, they find the wreck of a Jawa sandcrawler. Obi-Wan recognizes the work of Imperial stormtroopers, and realizes they were searching for the droids. Horrified, Luke returns to his family's homestead, only to find the Empire got there first and slaughtered his aunt and uncle. Devastated, Luke rejoins Kenobi and pledges to train as a Jedi, just like his father.

Luke. Kenobi, and the two droids travel to Mos Eisley spaceport where they meet smuggler Han Solo and his first mate, a giant Wookiee named Chewbacca, from whom they acquire transit aboard their

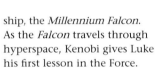

ship, the *Millennium Falcon*. As the *Falcon* travels through hyperspace, Kenobi gives Luke his first lesson in the Force.

On the Death Star, Grand Moff Tarkin attempts to make Leia reveal the location of the rebel base by threatening the destruction of her home planet, Alderaan. Leia complies (with a lie) but Tarkin orders the Death Star to open fire anyway, obliterating the planet.

Luke's training is interrupted after Kenobi senses a great disturbance in the Force. When the *Falcon* drops out of hyperspace and into a hail of debris there is no sign of their destination. Instead they are drawn towards what initially looks like a small moon, but is in fact a space station—the imposing Death Star!

The crew evade capture by hiding in the *Falcon*'s smuggling compartments, but in order to escape they need to deactivate the tractor beam that captured them. Kenobi takes on the task, but just after he leaves R2-D2 discovers that Princess Leia is being held in a detention block on the space station. Luke, Han, and Chewie head to the cell block and free the princess, before almost being crushed in a trash compactor. By now, stormtroopers have been alerted to their presence, and they split up to make their way back to the *Falcon*.

Kenobi, meanwhile, has successfully deactivated the tractor beam but is confronted by Darth Vader. Lightsabers drawn, they duel. When Kenobi sees Luke and his friends heading towards the *Falcon*, he lowers his blade and allows Vader to strike him down, distracting the Sith Lord from the fleeing rebels.

Blasting off and battling through a squadron of Imperial TIE fighters, the *Millennium Falcon* races to the rebel base on Yavin 4, unaware that they are being tracked by the Empire. After examining the technical readouts to the battle station, the rebels identify a weakness in the design that they can exploit—a small thermal exhaust port that, if hit, will cause a chain reaction that will destroy the deadly weapon.

As the Death Star closes in on the rebel base, a fleet of rebel starfighters engages with TIE fighters above the space station. Groups of X-wing and Y-wing fighters make several unsuccessful attempts to hit the exhaust port with proton torpedoes, until Luke Skywalker, pursued by Darth Vader, reaches out with his feelings, using the Force to guide his aim. His torpedo finds it's mark, and the Death Star explodes in a giant fireball.

The battle has been won, but the war is far from over.

01 Luke, Leia, and Han celebrate after the rebel's small but significant victory against the Empire's Death Star.

ACT TWO:

The stakes are are raised for the lead characters, who learn more about their capabilities as they strive to overcome many obstacles.

STAR WARS: THE EMPIRE STRIKES BACK

Searching for the new rebel base, the Empire dispatches thousands of probe droids across the galaxy. One lands on Hoth, the frozen planet where the rebels are hiding out. On patrol when the probe hits the ground, Luke Skywalker decides to investigate what he thinks is a meteorite strike, but before he can do so he is attacked by a wampa and dragged to its icy lair. Barely escaping with his life and lost in a snowstorm, Luke sees a vision of Obi-Wan Kenobi, who tells him to travel to Dagobah to find Yoda, a Jedi Master.

Rescued by Han Solo, Luke is recovering when Imperial ships are detected entering the Hoth system. Even though Solo and Chewbacca found and destroyed the probe droid, it had already revealed their

location to the Empire. Soon, rebel troops come under fire from approaching Imperial AT-AT walkers while Luke and his fellow pilots take on the all-but impregnable behemoths in snowspeeders.

Han Solo decides to get Leia to safety aboard the *Millennium Falcon* and, as snowtroopers close in, the ship blasts off into space—only to be immediately pursued by Star Destroyers. It's then that Han discovers the ship's hyperdrive is malfunctioning. His only option is to pilot the *Falcon* into an asteroid field, hoping to lose the TIE fighters closing in around them. Evading the Imperial ships, he hides the ship inside a large asteroid.

Luke leaves Hoth in his X-wing fighter with R2-D2, and they set course for Dagobah. The swampy planet seems totally inhospitable and not the kind of place to find a Jedi Master. After making camp, the rebel is surprised when a strange little figure arrives and begins going through his supplies. This, it transpires, is Yoda, and after some persuasion from the Force spirit of Obi-

Wan Kenobi, the old Jedi agrees to train young Skywalker.

Inside the asteroid cave, the *Falcon* crew are working feverishly to repair the ship's hyperdrive, although Han and Leia find time to share their first kiss. Unfortunately the cave in which Solo hid his ship turns out to be the gullet of a giant space slug, and they are forced to launch back into space, where the Empire is waiting. Once again the hyperdrive fails, but Han fakes an attack run on a Star Destroyer before using the *Falcon*'s landing claw to attach the ship to the rear of the Imperial vessel's conning tower.

Determined to capture the *Millennium Falcon,* Darth Vader has employed the services of bounty hunters to track it down, including Boba Fett. It is Fett who recognizes Han's maneuver and is waiting when Solo detaches his ship and lets it float away amid the Star Destroyer's dumped garbage.

The *Falcon* arrives at Bespin and lands on Cloud City, where an old friend of Han and Chewie's is the administrator, Lando Calrissian. At first, he doesn't seem best pleased by

02 The rebels on the run from a relentless Imperial pursuit.

03 Luke undergoes intensive training with Yoda.

04 Lando Calrissian checks on the health of his old buddy, Han Solo.

05 Darth Vader tries to tempt Luke by making a terrifying confession.

03

04

05

the arrival of Solo, but the suave scoundrel breaks a smile and warmly welcomes Han and his friends.

However, all is not as it seems. C-3PO goes missing, while Leia remains suspicious of Calrissian—and with good reason. Invited to dinner by Lando, it transpires that the real host is Darth Vader, with Boba Fett at his side. The Empire arrived shortly before the *Millennium Falcon*, and Calrissian was forced into making a deal with Vader in order to maintain control of his mining operation. But Han, Leia, and the others are merely bait to draw Luke Skywalker into a trap. Vader plans to capture and deliver Luke to the Emperor, who has recognized the boy's potential, and has Han Solo frozen in a block of carbonite to ensure the process will be safe to use on Skywalker.

Meanwhile, during training on Dagobah, Luke senses the plight of his friends and decides he must to rush to their aid, despite Yoda and Obi-Wan's protestations.

When Luke arrives on Cloud City, he finds Vader waiting for him in the carbon-freezing chamber, and they begin a duel. Skywalker is clearly outmatched, and Vader forces him to the edge of a gantry and disarms his opponent before revealing a terrible truth to the boy: "*I* am your Father." Given a choice between joining Vader on the dark side or death, Luke allows himself to fall from the gantry.

With the Empire taking over the city, Lando switches sides and releases Leia, Chewie, and C-3PO before they are taken to Vader's ship. They attempt to stop Boba Fett leaving with the frozen Solo but are unsuccessful, and instead flee on the *Falcon*, pausing only to rescue Luke, dangling from an antennae beneath the city.

Safely back with the rebel fleet, Lando and Chewbacca leave on a mission to find Han Solo. ☻

RETURN OF THE JEDI

Arriving in theaters on May 25, 1983, *Star Wars: Return of the Jedi* was the very definition of a final act. The plot threads left hanging at the end of *The Empire Strikes Back* would be tied up, the constant threat posed by the Empire across the previous two movies would be overcome forever, and the lead characters would find themselves transformed and facing a brighter future.

ACT THREE:

In which the story reaches new levels of tension before the resolution, bringing the central plot and various subplots to a satisfying conclusion.

A long time ago, in a galaxy far, far away....

Luke Skywalker has returned to his home planet of Tatooine in an attempt to rescue his friend Han Solo from the clutches of the vile gangster Jabba the Hutt.

Little does Luke know that the Galactic Empire has secretly begun construction on a new armored space station even more powerful than the first dreaded Death Star.

When completed, this ultimate weapon will spell certain doom for the small band of rebels struggling to restore freedom to the galaxy...

-3PO and R2-D2 present themselves to Jabba the Hutt as gifts from Jedi Knight Luke Skywalker, who issues a holographic threat to Jabba—release Han Solo or die. An attempt to rescue Solo by Princess Leia, disguised as a bounty hunter, is discovered and she and Chewie also become the Hutt's prisoners. When Luke eventually arrives in Jabba's court, he too is captured after defeating Jabba's pet rancor, and sentenced to death in the belly of the almighty Sarlacc alongside Solo.

However, this was all part of Luke's plan to rescue his friend. When they arrive at the Pit of Carkoon aboard Jabba's sail barge, R2-D2 fires Luke's lightsaber skyward, where the Jedi uses the Force to draw it into his hand, and a battle ensues, resulting in the death of Jabba at the hands of Leia and

the destruction of the sail barge. Lando Calrissian pilots a skiff carrying Luke, Leia, Han, Chewie, and the droids to safety and they leave Tatooine far behind them.

As the *Millennium Falcon* heads off to rejoin the rebel fleet, Luke travels to Dagobah where he finds Yoda sick and dying. To Luke's shock, Yoda reveals that there is another Skywalker before he fades away and becomes one with the Force. The spirit of Obi-Wan Kenobi confirms that Luke has a sister, and Skywalker senses it is none other than Leia. Kenobi warns him to hide this knowledge from Darth Vader, whom he must confront once again.

Aboard the rebel flagship *Home One*, Mon Mothma and Admiral Ackbar reveal the existence of a second Death Star, and that the Emperor himself is overseeing its construction. They unveil a plan to destroy the new superweapon and the Empire with one strike.

01

General Han Solo leads a strike team to the Forest Moon of Endor, where their mission is to shut down the defensive shield protecting the new Death Star above the planet. However, the team becomes separated when Imperial scout troopers spot the rebels and take off on speeder bikes. Leia and Luke set off in pursuit and take out the troopers, but Leia goes missing. Han, Luke, Chewie, and the droids set out to find her, only to be captured by an indigenous tribe of Ewoks. Leia befriends one of the creatures who found her unconscious in the forest. The friends are reunited in the the Ewok's Bright Tree Village and gain the trust of the tribe, who offer to help the rebels.

Luke fears he is endangering the mission and decides to leave, but not before revealing his kinship to Leia and the truth of their parentage. Luke tells his sister that he can sense the good in Vader, and after leaving the village he surrenders to the Imperial troopers and is brought before his father. Vader insists it is too late for him to be saved, and instructs his troops to take Luke to the awaiting shuttle for transport to the Emperor.

The Ewoks know of a secret back door to the Imperial bunker housing the defense shield, and cause a distraction allowing the rebels to enter the structure, and Han and his comrades begin planting explosives. Meanwhile, on the Death Star II, the Emperor tells Luke that he is aware of the rebel plan.

As the Alliance's fleet drops out of hyperspace and moves into attack formation, Imperial troopers capture the rebels in the bunker on Endor, leaving the shield still raised. At the last moment, Admiral Ackbar recognizes it's a trap, and Lando Calrissian commands all ships to take evasive action.

Far from being incomplete, the Emperor's new Death Star is fully armed and operational, and it begins firing on the fleet. This is all too much for Luke, who

02

grabs his lightsaber and attempts to strike down the Emperor, only to have his blow met by Darth Vader's red blade.

The Ewoks mount a counterattack against the Imperial troops, and the rebels are once again able to enter the base and replant their bombs. This time their efforts are rewarded when the base explodes and the defensive shield is destroyed. In space, Lando pilots the *Millennium Falcon* into the Death Star's infrastructure and locates the station's main reactor core. Proton torpedoes fired from the *Falcon* and Wedge Antilles' X-wing find their mark, and a chain reaction begins.

Meanwhile, Luke and Vader's duel becomes more intense after the Sith Lord senses Luke's secret. Enraged, Luke launches a ferocious attack on Vader and

the laughing Emperor, pleased to have found a new apprentice, insists he finishes the job. Luke composes himself and throws away his lightsaber, unwilling to turn to the dark side. The Emperor punishes him with an onslaught of Force-generated lighting, but Darth Vader cannot allow his son to be killed and hurls his master into an abyss and to his apparent doom. Dying due to the Sith energy he absorbed, Vader asks Luke to remove his helmet, and father and son share a peaceful moment together before the former Jedi dies.

The Death Star II explodes in a huge fireball. The Empire has been defeated and celebrations ensue across the galaxy, including on Endor where the victorious rebel heroes are finally reunited. ☙

01 Publicity image of Harrison Ford (Han Solo), Carrie Fisher (Princess Leia), and Mark Hamill (Luke Skywalker) on location in Northern California. (Previous spread)

02 Solo: ready for action!

03 The droids and the Ewoks find themselves under fire from Imperial stormtroopers.

04 Father and son, together for the last time.

03

04

WRITING AND PRE-PRODUCTION

For all the kinetic action, adventure, dazzling effects, and rollercoaster emotions of *Return of the Jedi*, the movie began as pencil notes on sheets of lined yellow notepaper, as George Lucas tried to coral ideas that had been percolating in his imagination for almost a decade.

Some of Lucas' early *Jedi* outlines were more rough notes, detailing ideas such as Yoda and Ben Kenobi helping Luke to rescue Han Solo, the *Millennium Falcon* being taken by an "angry landlord," and "Ewaks" dressing up Leia. A second outline went into more detail, splitting the story into three acts, each of which would be comprised of 15 scenes across a 90-page script. He drew upon earlier ideas he'd originally devised for *A New Hope*, including the expansive land battle that would form part of the movie's climax.

"I had to fill in a lot of blanks for *Jedi* from a lot of things that had been added into this one by the two previous films," Lucas had stated. "The whole story had really been about a primitive society overcoming the Empire at the end… In the original script, [that] was really only the last 20 pages. So I had to come up with another hundred pages of stuff and make it work. I wandered in all kinds of directions, trying to avoid those things which were in the very first rough draft, but it turned out better just to say, 'Forget it. It sounds redundant, but we'll do it again.'"

Pre-production moved forward while Lucas was still writing, but the filmmaker had enough ideas to give concept artists Ralph McQuarrie, Nilo Rodis-Jamero, and Joe Johnston something to work with. Soon, designs for the Imperial capital of Had Abbadon, a grass planet, rocket bikes, Ewoks, and Jabba the Hutt were being conceptualized—all without the benefit of a script to work from.

"George said we were to make it up as we go, graphically. It was a free-for-all, a very friendly competition," said Rodis-Jamero. "Every two weeks, George would sit down and as quickly as you could put down images, he would either mark it with a red dot, or not."

A coveted red dot saw a concept approved for further development.

"We don't worry about how they are going to work or how they are going to be built or photographed," said Joe Johnston. "We just do what we think would look the best on the screen."

With *Revenge of the Jedi* having been announced as the film's title (which would only be amended to *"Return"* during post production), and principal photography scheduled to begin in the fall of 1981, Lucas had begun transforming his outlines into a full-length script. He would write in his office from 9 a.m. to 6 p.m. every day for weeks.

02

leather

01 Director Richard
Marquand and
co-producer Robert
Watts on the *Home
One* set. Watts wears
a jacket issued to
crewmembers working
on *The Empire Strikes
Back*. (Previous spread)

02 A costume
breakdown chart
was used by the
"plastic boys" to track
the components of
the scout trooper
costume they were
responsible for.

COSTUME

IMPERIAL BIKE RIDER   QTY: 12

396 PCS TOTAL

PART	MATERIAL	PROCESS	FINISH	FABRICATION	ASSEMBLY
HELMET TOP	ABS	VAC FORM			
HELMET SIDES (2)	ABS	VAC FORM		BOND SIDES TO HELMET TOP	
VISOR	ABS	VAC FORM / STRIP HEAT			FRICTION HINGE TO HELMET ASS'Y
~~LENS~~	ACRYLIC	VAC FORM	POLISH	BOND TO FACE PLATE	
FACE PLATE	~~ABS~~	VAC FORM		BOND TO VISOR	
BREAST PLATE	~~ABS~~	VAC FORM			VELCRO ?
~~SHOULDER~~	ABS	VAC. FORM			
BELT #1	ABS /	VAC FORM		CUT SLOTS FOR WEB	
BELT #2 (2)	STD BELT				
GUN CRADLE (2)	~~ABS~~	VAC FORM		CUT SLOTS FOR WEB	
LEG PCS. (2)	ABS	VAC FORM			FIX TO FABRIC
BACK PLATE	ABS	VAC FORM			
KNEE GUARD (2)	ABS	VAC FORM			

03

#2

①

Act I

1 Vader meets moff jerjerrod - (trap?)

2 Vader + Jer Jerrod establish moon - (parry)

3 Moon Robots meets Leia + rebels news of Luke. - R-2 (later - Leia upset) must see Leia alone-upset 3PO

4 Vader meet emperor.

5 Moff + Emperor talks.

6 Vader Contact luke

7 Luke yoda talk — establish end (vader)

8 Leia + R-2 talk — send after Luke — 3PO puzzled. - watched.

9 Vader — death star — clue —

10 Emperor plan.

11 Luke — yoda dies. — must forgive Ben — Establish end (Vader)

12 Luke bury yoda — talk with Ben — establish end (Vader)

13 Robots arrive at Degobah — meet luke take off - Leia - meet you on alliance planet. meeting of all rebels. mission almost complete.

14 Vader on moon. — Leia watch — ray gun captured

15 Leia — chased. rocket cycle - escape - thrown unconscious.

03 George Lucas's handwritten notes for the first act of *Return of the Jedi*.

04 Designs for a biker scout and Lando's disguise by Nilo Rodis-Jamero.

BIKER. MJR 7.81. ©LFL

LANDO'S DISGUISE MJR 7.81 ©LFL

02

04

George Lucas had initially believed that Harrison Ford might not return as Han Solo as the actor was only contractually obligated to appear in *A New Hope* and *The Empire Strikes Back*. Producer Howard Kazanjian stepped in, swiftly negotiating a new deal.

As with *Empire*, a new director was sought. Impressed by Richard Marquand's film *Eye of the Needle* (1981), Lucas hired the director beating other contenders such as David Lynch, Richard Donner, Richard Attenborough, Tony Scott, and John Glen, who

by this point had served as assistant director on two *James Bond* movies.

Following his success scripting *The Empire Strikes Back,* Lawrence Kasdan had moved on. His debut as a director, *Body Heat* (1981) was produced in part thanks to help from Lucas. As a favor to the man who had been instrumental in establishing his career, Kasdan agreed to pen the new *Star Wars* film that was already well into pre-production. He later reflected that, "The process for *Jedi* was the same as *Empire*—we were

already a speeding train. There were designs and pictures of things before I even started writing. George was relieved when I came onboard because I was going to do the part he hated, so he could concentrate on the part he loved, which was to design and produce."

Lucas welcomed the collaboration, stating, "The script is something where you work with artists and say 'I have some ideas, now you give me some ideas and we'll go back and forth and put them all together and see what happens....'"

THE SECOND DEATH STAR

The Emperor's plan to use a new Death Star to lure the rebel fleet into a trap provided the central plot device for *Return of the Jedi*, but in George Lucas' early story outlines for the film there were not one but *two* Death Stars.

n the opening crawl from Lucas' rough draft for *Revenge of the Jedi*, dated February 24, 1981, it states that, "The rebellion is doomed. Spies loyal to the Old Republic have sent word of two new armored space stations under construction." During pre-production, concept art by Ralph McQuarrie depicted this duo of Death Stars in orbit around a city planet named Had Abbadon, the Emperor's seat of power. But as the storyline was refined, it was decided that two superweapons overcomplicated the plot, and that a single, incomplete Death Star provided a more achievable target for the rebels—and the perfect bait in the Emperor's trap.

A matte painting of the incomplete Death Star had been made, but Lucas felt it didn't offer enough options for composing the shots he wanted. A model was therefore commissioned, which turned out to be one of the most intricate miniatures built for the movie, using acid-etched brass to create the multiple levels of unfinished infrastructure in the design.

The 240-foot long set for the Death Star hangar was built on Stage 6 at Elstree, at an estimated cost of $750,000. Fifty new stormtrooper costumes were made to bolster the Imperial ranks for the scene of the Emperor's arrival, which were increased vastly in a matte painting of the hanger by artist Frank Ordaz. Another matte painting, by Chris Evans, of the exterior of the docking bay entrances around the Death Star's circumference, was photographed using a technique called Auto Matte, which combined paintings with miniatures in the foreground to add further dimensionality to a matte shot. ☻

01

01 The second Death Star is revealed.
02 A detailed look at the incomplete battle station.

04

03 A nervous Moff Jerjerrod greets Vader.

04 A fresh set of approximately 50 stormtrooper units was manufactured for *Return of the Jedi*. The costumes were photographed as pristine white outfits in the Death Star sequences, which were shot first, and later dirtied down for use in filming Endor sequences on location.

THE COURT OF JABBA THE HUTT

The shadowy throne room of Jabba the Hutt was filled with a dizzying array of creatures, from familiar Jawas and Rodians to wilder new characters such as Bib Fortuna, Max Rebo, and Sy Snootles. The smokey, atmospheric lighting lent the chamber its salubrious vibe, but the enclosed set—packed with puppets, performers, and crew—made it a difficult place to work.

 ithout any question, the hardest scene in every way was Jabba's palace," said director Richard Marquand. "It was a very, very crowded set. It was incredibly hot. There were a lot of extras and a lot of crew, and nobody could take a break, so everybody ended up on the set all the time. Between takes the noise was infernal."

Temperatures could reach more than 100 degrees under the studio lights, and the crew had to be mindful of the wellbeing of the creature performers buried beneath heavy latex masks. People were always on hand with refreshments and fans to keep them as cool as possible between takes.

"The range of creatures in Jabba's palace did compound my problems," said production designer Norman Reynolds, "because it meant that the entire set had to be built up off the floor in order to accommodate the people who would be working the creatures from below."

With little room to maneuver in the cramped set, it was important that everyone knew where they had to be during a take. Each creature was assigned two positions in the throne room where they would be placed for different scenes, and each set-up was planned like a theatrical play, with characters entering, moving to their mark, and performing their lines. Unusually, Marquand chose to film all the scenes set in the throne room in story order rather than out of sequence.

Of all the exotic creatures in the palace, Jabba's Majordomo Bib Fortuna was the only one with any major dialogue (apart from the Hutt himself), although his look alone was striking enough to make him stand out. The makeup, designed by Stuart Freeborn, consisted of foam latex appliances specific to actor Michael Carter's face, some of which could inflate and deflate to add to Fortuna's alien appearance. A chin waddle and two long tentacles extended from his head, making him look even less human. The design was so complicated that Carter endured eight hours in the makeup chair every day.

Among the other notable new creatures were the Gamorrean "pig" guards, with their expressive snouts and frowns, which were achieved via a system of cables built into their masks and operated by wire by an off-camera puppeteer. Many of Jabba's court were operated in this way, usually with a performer inside a costume to provide the more physical attributes of the character.

02

03

Working on the set proved uncomfortable for Femi Taylor, who played Oola, Jabba's ill-fated dancer. Taylor, who would return to film extra material for the 1997 *Return of the Jedi* special edition, was nearly strangled by Jabba's chain on numerous occassions by puppeteers who had limited visibility. Thankfully Mark Hamill kept an eye on her and made sure she was okay.

Jeremy Bulloch, returning as Boba Fett, used his time on set to appear as deadly but subtle as possible, "I would be thinking, *Is he suitable prey?* and I would move forward very gently. I loved playing around. I'd think, *Is there something I can do in this scene to look cool?*"

Sy Snootles, the featured singer at the palace, was a marionette operated by Tim Rose who performed double duty manipulating Salacious. B. Crumb. "Instead of being controlled from above, Snootles floated in the air and was pulled down to the ground by rods and wires She was very hard to control and I could only get a good take once every 12 attempts. When it came time to shoot I was only given two takes to get it right, neither of which were very good. I think that's proabably why she was replaced by CGI for the re-releases."

Filming on the set proved hazardous for a certain crewmember as Anthony Daniels recalls, "Jabba knocks Threepio over. An unamed crewmember was asked to hold the padded board that I was due to fall onto. However, the crewmember took a blow to the face from Threepio's elbow as he fell. He was henceforth known as 'Scar*chin*!'"

Despite the discomfort of the set, Anthony Daniels remarked, "It looked good on the screen, and that's what counts in the end." ☢

01 Bib Fortuna and a selection of creatures from the palace. (Previous spread)

02 The Max Rebo Band perform for Jabba and his courtiers. Original production art by Ralph McQuarrie.

03 Femi Taylor as Oola.

04

05

07

06

04 C-3PO finds himself working for Jabba the Hutt.

05 Jabba's prize.

06 Luke bargains for the life of his friend.

07 The Max Rebo Band entertain Jabba.

08 The mysterious bounty hunter Boushh arrives with a captive Chewbacca.

09 Boba Fett stands ready for action.

08

09

JABBA THE HUTT

Audiences had been waiting to see Jabba the Hutt ever since his name was casually mentioned in *A New Hope.* Now, with a carbonite-encased Han Solo displayed as a trophy on his wall and our heroes mounting a bold rescue, the time was right to finally meet the vile gangster.

 A udiences first heard the name "Jabba the Hutt" during the infamous Han Solo versus Greedo Cantina encounter in *A New Hope,* and they almost got to see the him in the movie too, had budgetary constraints not interfered.

Belfast-born actor Declan Mulholland was filmed in the role of Jabba, and George Lucas' original plan was to replace the on-set actor with some kind of VFX monster. Although the Jabba scene was filmed at Elstree Studios in London (allowing it to be reinstated years later for the Special Edition), Mulholland's performance ended up on the cutting-room floor.

Jabba was resurrected for *Return of the Jedi*, this time in the form of an enormous puppet. The character's omission from *A New Hope* meant that artists including Phil Tippett, Nilo Rodis-Jamero, Ken Ralston, and Ralph McQuarrie could let their imaginations run wild when designing the vile gangster. Having explored numerous takes on the character, the form of a repulsive, slug-like creature imagined by Tippett was chosen by Lucas and further refined.

The task of creating the puppet itself fell to Stuart Freeborn's creature-shop team in London, and the Hutt was sculpted by John Coppinger under Freeborn's direction.

"Jabba was enormous, one of the most difficult ones," Freeborn revealed. "It took four tons of clay. I had the carpenters construct a frame and then we modeled the clay over the wooden structure. We tried to make him so evil."

The completed Hutt was finished just in time for filming, having cost nearly $500,000 to fabricate over three months.

The puppet was complex, with fully articulated eyes that could convey a range of emotions, an expressive mouth with a prehensile tongue, and the ability to eat and drink. Consequently it required several operators to bring Jabba to life. Chief puppeteer David Barclay operated Jabba's right arm and jaw, relaying the Hutt's dialogue in English during filming; Toby Philpott operated Jabba's left arm and head, along with his slimy tongue; and Mike Edmonds (who also portrayed Logray the Ewok in the film) was tasked with flicking the gangster's tail in tune with the Hutt's emotional state.

"Like so many puppets and animatronics, those first few hours of bringing the character to life seemed almost impossible," said Dave Barclay of operating the giant creature. "But with rehearsal and watching back the video tapes of the movements, our bodies got used to the unique physical requirements of the role. We suddenly began to feel at home inside Jabba, which is just as well, as we spent nearly 10 hours a day inside of him!" ☻

01 Jabba the Hutt is finally revealed.

02 Leia is subjected
to Jabba's questionable
"charms."

03 Early concepts of
Jabba as illustrated
by Ralph McQuarrie.

04 Creature creator
Phil Tippett (right)
supervises as Jabba's
right arm grabs a frog!

02

03

THE RANCOR

Those unfortunate enough to have upset, let down, or angered the volatile Jabba the Hutt could look forward to a brief encounter with the rancor, the carnivorous monster that dwelled in a cave-like enclosure beneath the crime lord's throne room. The green-skinned Twi'lek dancer Oola and an unlucky Gamorrean guard both met grizzly ends in the jaws of the creature, and Luke Skywalker barely escaped its clutches with his life.

Initially, the rancor creature was to have been realized by a performer wearing a 15-foot tall costume, and a prototype was built from foam and latex in the production's U.S. Monster Shop at ILM in San Rafael, overseen by Phil Tippett. "George was really adamant that we were going to do it as a man in a suit," Tippett recalled. "It was going to be like a really cool *Godzilla*."

The sequence was meticulously planned, and Dennis Muren filmed and edited a videomatic of the entire scene to enable the crew at Elstree Studios to visualize and capture every shot that was required. However, it quickly became apparent that the creature suit route was not going to work. "George just didn't care for it at all," said Muren. "When he saw the footage, he thought that it really wasn't getting anywhere and told us to go ahead and try it any other way we wanted."

The ILM crew changed tack. Without the time or budget to use the Go-motion technique Tippett had originally suggested (devised to add realistic blur to the stop-motion animated tauntauns and AT-ATs of *The Empire Strikes Back*), they opted instead to use a rod-operated rancor puppet inspired by Japanese Bunraku puppetry, which was then filmed at very high speed to give the illusion of scale.

Over on the soundstage at Elstree in London, three life-sized cutouts made of wood stood in for the rancor on set, so that Mark Hamill (Luke Skywalker) and the camera operator could envisage where the creature was supposed to be during each take.

"I had an amazing encounter with this 30-foot creature, the rancor, who wasn't there at all," said Hamill after filming was completed. "In shooting that sequence, one of my biggest acting dreams came true: I actually got to be held in a giant rubber hand." ☻

02

03

04

01 The rancor: terror below the palace.

02 The movable rancor maquette as used in the film.

03 An unfortunate Gammorean finds itself on the menu.

04 Luke Skywalker prepares to defend himself.

05 The rancor versus Luke Skywalker. Original production art by Ralph McQuarrie.

INTO THE SARLACC PIT

Having condemned Luke Skywalker and Han Solo to a slow death in the stomach of the almighty Sarlacc, Jabba the Hutt gathered his entourage onto his personal sail barge and set off into Tatooine's Dune Sea. Rather than returning to Tunisia, which had doubled for the desert planet in *A New Hope*, the *Return of the Jedi* crew found a location that was closer to home.

"Buttercup Valley" doesn't sound like the kind of place one would expect to find an ever-changing landscape of sand dunes, but that's exactly what the arid location outside Yuma offered, making it a perfect fit for the Sarlacc Pit sequence. "Truth of it is, Tunisia doesn't have very many sand dunes, which means we'd have to go into Algeria, or some other place," George Lucas once stated. "In Algeria the dunes are 1,200 miles from the nearest civilization. In Yuma, they're close to hotels."

Close, but far enough away that the production had to construct a two-mile temporary road linking the closest highway to the filming location, enabling them to ferry in the huge amount of material required to build the sail barge and the Great Pit of Carkoon set.

The barge itself was 150-feet long and 65-feet high, set upon a 30,000-square-foot platform housing the pit and a skiff, all of which were raised 27 feet above the desert floor. Providing a stable foundation for the set, 130 wooden poles were driven into the ground. The barge's immense red sails were made from 4,000 square feet of polyester material sewn with triple stitching and reinforced with corner panels. The entire build was budgeted at $400,000.

Designer Joe Johnston made the sail barge and it's attendant skiffs look they originated from the same culture, explained that, "the skiffs are almost like lifeboats from the barge."

Making the best use of the vast space between the wooden posts underneath the set, a host of offices, storage areas, and a commissary (to feed the shoot's army of cast and crewmembers) were built, providing some

much-needed shade from the intense heat outside. Nearby, out in the desert, a production office and medical center were hidden from view, disguised as sand dunes.

When local word got out that the horror film *Blue Harvest*, which was filming in the desert, was actually a *Star Wars* movie, a fence had to be created around its perimeter to deter interlopers, such as fans, bikers, and dune-buggy enthusiasts, from descending on the set. Production was further hampered by stormy weather, which repeatedly blew sand off of the Sarlacc pit set, leaving its wooden frame visible.

Two skiffs were made, one situated at ground level, making it safer to film stunts. "The best decision we made was to have a second skiff," Richard Marquand said. "We we were able to do all of the closeup stuff on zip-up platforms

01 The heroes face execution at the Sarlacc pit.

02 Jabba's foes face death at the Great Pit of Carkoon.
Original production art by Ralph McQuarrie.

03

around it. That was money well spent, because there was very little danger there."

A second skiff was made to tilt on cue to simulate being hit by blaster fire from the barge's rail-mounted cannon.

Jabba's henchmen got their distinctive names from a variety of sources. The Weequay species' name came from the character Queequag from Herman Melville's *Moby Dick*. Originally referred to as Queequay by the crew, the name was altered by the time the character was turned into an action figure. Klaatu, Barada, and Nikto were named after a key phrase used in the science fiction movie *The Day the Earth Stood Still* (1951).

The launch of Luke's lightsaber from R2-D2's dome took several takes until the lightweight prop flew satisfactorily from the droid. The lightsaber hilt, brandished by the Jedi as he fought off Jabba's

henchmen was originally one of Obi-Wan's fighting props from *A New Hope*. before being used in practice sessions for the climactic duel in *The Empire Strikes Back*.

During the battle, one of Jabba's unlucky henchmen issues a familiar cry. Sound designer Ben Burtt used one of his favorite Easter eggs, the "Wilhelm Scream" to accompany the bad guy's fall into the mouth of the Sarlacc.

Amidst the chaos of the battle was final showdown between Han Solo and Boba Fett. The bounty hunter is armed with an updated version of his blaster rifle as seen in *The Empire Strikes Back*. While still based on the same First World War-era flare gun with an air rifle scope on top, new details from were added and the barrel ridged with the same grip material as Darth Vader's lightsaber. Several copies were made for the shoot, including a

break-apart pyrotechnic blaster.

Jabba's demise at the hands of Leia was inspired by a scene in *The Godfather* (1972), directed by George Lucas's friend Francis Ford Coppola. The sequence in which Luca Brasi, a corpulant gangster is strangled to death with a piano wire is echoed when the captive princess uses her chains to choke her captor.

Versatile stunt performer Tracy Eddon wore a rubber replica of C-3PO's costume in order to perform the droid's tumble over the side of the sail barge. She then donned the iconic metal bikini to perform a more dignified escape from the barge as she swung to freedom with Mark Hamill's double.

After filming was completed, the lumber used in the construction of the set was sold as salvage, and Lucasfilm returned the location to the same condition it had been in when they arrived.

A scene that immediately followed the battle was ultimately cut from the movie. As the heroes return to their ships, a sandstorm whirls around them. The scene was the first to be filmed for the production but was beset by difficulties when R2-D2 crashed into a rock, the camera crew couldn't hear their director over the wind machine, and flying sand made visibillty practically non-existant.

The 1997 Special Edition release of *Return of the Jedi* saw numerous enhancements made to the original film. As the vehicles propel themselves across the desert, a herd of banthas, creatures last seen transporting sand people in *A New Hope*, can be seen walking across the sand. The Sarlacc itself gained a ferocious beak. ☮

03 The heroes face an uncertain fate.

04 Luke prepares to leap into action. The creature's threatening beak was added for the 1997 Special Edition of the movie.

05 The full-sized *Millennium Falcon* on set for the ultimately abandoned sandstorm sequence. This would have been the only time in the movie that a practical 1:1 version of the ship would be seen. (Following spread)

THE EMPEROR

Mentioned in *A New Hope*, and only seen in the form of a hologram in *The Empire Strikes Back*, the Emperor was an important yet peripheral figure in the *Star Wars* galaxy until he made his full presence felt in *Return of the Jedi*.

"We spent a long, long time casting the Emperor," said Richard Marquand of the search for someone to portray the ultimate evil in the cosmos. Many well respected actors read for the part, including Sir Ben Kingsley, but the producers were undecided as to whether an older performer with a lifetime of experience was better suited to the role, or if they should cast someone younger.

Initially Alan Webb landed the part, a 75 year-old actor with a decades-long career behind him, but he had to pull out due to illness. 35 year-old Ian McDiarmid was cast in his place, and a cinematic icon was born.

"Mary Selway, the casting director, had seen me in a play called *Seduced*. I played a character many years older than my own age." Selway suggested the actor to George Lucas and Richard Marquand who cast McDiarmid after a brief meeting. To transform the youthful McDiarmid into the ancient Emperor, an extensive makeup was applied, giving the character a hideously ancient and scarred appearance. Contact lenses gave the Emperor his piercing glare, but it was McDiarmid's icy performance that brought the character to life.

"During any breaks in the shoot, I just sat in my room, surrounded by mirrors," McDiarmid recollected. "I saw this creature staring at me, and I did, I'm afraid, spend a great deal of time just looking at this thing that we had all created."

The makeup up application would initially take four hours but this was reduced to two and a half as filming progressed. For the actor's comfort, crewmembers would pass drinks which he could sip through a straw between takes. Eating was a challenge but the makeup artist, Nick Dudman, offered to retouch the mouth area.

Mark Hamill, whose makeup as Luke Skywalker was more strightforward, realized that he would never see his what his co-star actually looked like. Inviting to his house for a Sunday dinner, Hamill was surpised to meet a much younger man with a shock of red hair.

As he observed the physical attributes of the persona he was to inhabit, McDiarmid began to consider how he should sound. However, Richard Marquand asked him to mimic the performance given by Clive Revill, who had voiced the Emperor in *The Empire Strikes Back*.

"Clive Revill was great, but he didn't really know the character he was playing," the actor said. Having spent time with the Emperor's face, McDiarmid knew he had to sound quite different.

"When I saw the face in the mirror, I thought, my God, it looks like Somerset Maugham, who's turned into a toad," said McDiarmid. "So, the voice became a combination of English upper class and trying to sound like a toad. I thought it had to come from somewhere deep down."

02

01 The Emperor arrives
aboard the partially
completed Death Star.
(Previous spread)

02 The Emperor's royal
guards flank two of his
closest advisors, Sim
Aloo (Anthony Lang)
and Janus Greejatus
(Michael Josephs) in
this publicity shot.

03 Makeup artist Nick Dudman transforms Ian McDiarmid into the evil Emperor.

04 The mysterious Sith Lord, known only at this stage as the Emperor.

McDiarmid spent 13 days on set as the Emperor, and re-recorded his dialogue at Mayflower Recording Studios the following January.

"We dubbed over a four-day period, with lots of breaks in between, and that's very good because, especially in a film, it allows you to refine your performance," said McDiarmid. During post-production, sound editor Ben Burtt added reverb and echo effects to lend an extra creepiness to the actor's performance.

The actor found the Emperor's lines to be "fun and simple. They don't really have any subtext. If you wield that kind of power, you don't have to bother with subtext, you just say and enact what you feel.

The Emperor's strength is that he is not fearful."

While the Emperor specializes in terror, the actor behind the performance is far more affable, able to enjoy a laugh with castmates between takes with his fellow actors, "although when I laughed it hurt because of the makeup!"

Of the Emperor's grandiose entrance into the film, director Richard Marquand recalled, "It's a wonderful moment in the film when the Emperor comes out of the shuttle. It's astonishing. The robes of the red troops. But you're talking about filming 200 people and you're watching the main action—when you suddenly notice there's a guy who is still putting his helmet on, so you have to go again?"

McDiarmid recalled, "I was taken up to this high scaffold. They pointed me in the right direction and, suddenly, there was steam and smoke. The ramp shot down and all these people in red and black preceded me. A voice said, 'Cue Emperor!' and I hobbled down."

"I saw the film with some four-year-old children who I know," McDiarmid later said. "They wouldn't believe that I was the Emperor of the Universe. I said, 'I'm Darth Vader's boss,' but they wouldn't have any of it. Then, halfway through the movie they realized it must be true. By the end of the film, they sat there looking stunned and wouldn't speak to me. They wouldn't come anywhere near me!" ☻

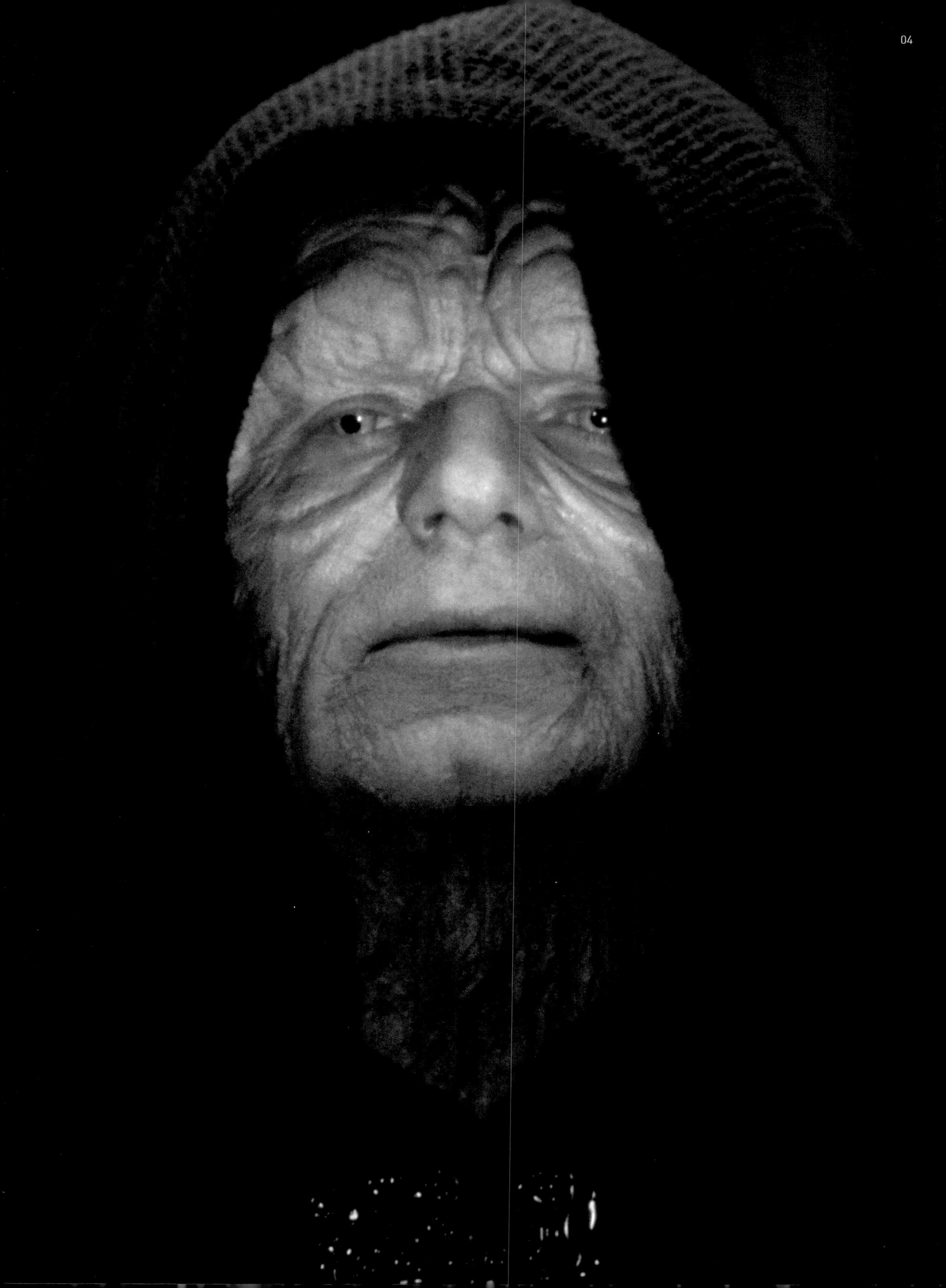

RETURN TO DAGOBAH

Having begun his Jedi training under Obi-Wan Kenobi in *A New Hope*, and learned more about the Force thanks to Yoda in *The Empire Strikes Back*, Luke Skywalker had unfinished business with both masters, requiring a return visit to the swamps of Dagobah.

As Dagobah played a smaller role in *Jedi*, the set was commensurately smaller in scale than the one built for *The Empire Strikes Back*, consisting of a section of forest containing both Yoda's hut, a pool, and Luke's X-wing fighter. Conditions were even more cramped inside the Jedi's home, which had to accommodate Mark Hamill as Skywalker, the Yoda puppet, and the puppeteers who operated him from beneath the set's floor.

Delays in the construction of two new Yoda puppets meant that Frank Oz, who reprised his role as the Jedi Master, had been rehearsing with a stand-in puppet. The *Jedi* Yoda was based on the molds from *Empire* with some cosmetic changes and improved limbs and joints. However, "We had problems with [Yoda's] eyes," revealed Marquand. "Suddenly they would stick on one side or the other. But because Yoda is a very old man and on his death bed, you feel, well, his eyes can go slightly off center."

Sir Alec Guinness had returned to portray Obi-Wan Kenobi, although he was suffering from the after effects of flu during his two days on set.

"Guinness had asked for some script changes so he could say lines in his Ben Kenobi style," said director Marquand. "George went to his house on a Saturday, and they spent the day together and talked about the part. In fact, what he and George worked out was very, very good indeed." ☸

01

01 Luke returns to Dagobah to seek advice from an ailing Yoda.

02 Yoda confirms Luke's greatest fear during the Jedi Master's final moments.

03 Kenobi relays his story. Note that the shimmering "Force spirit" effect has yet to be added. (Following spread)

04 Sir Alec Guinness contributed to the script to ensure that Kenobi's dialogue was authentic. (Following spread)

HOME ONE

When the rebel fleet amassed at Sullust to prepare for its assault on the second Death Star, *Home One* acted as its primary command vessel, under the command of Admiral Ackbar.

 nlike the harsh, geometric starship designs favored by the Imperials, Mon Calamari vessels were far more organic in shape, elongated and sleek, with pods of different sizes along the length of their hulls.

Industrial Light & Magic modelmakers constructed the command ship, which they christened "the pickle ship," based on a 16-inch maquette, sculpted by Lorne Peterson.

"I started out with three big blocks of basswood," said modelmaker Ira Keeler. "Those were split from bottom to top, and then shaped. Then I made these little bumps from pieces of battered wood, in all different shapes and sizes, vacuum formed them, and added them onto the ship. When that was all set up as a pattern, a mold was made and the miniature was cast out of fiberglass. I drilled little holes in the paint for the windows, so the light from a neon bulb inside would show through. By the time we were done, the model was eight feet long, so I had to sit it on two garbage cans to work on it. It was a big, big job."

At one point, executive producer George Lucas visited the model shop to see how the cruiser was progressing. "I had a piece of wood laid out to cut it down and shape it, and George said, 'Are you making a surfboard?'" recalled Keeler. "Yeah, pretty much yeah, I was!"

The live-action sequences set in the ship's main briefing room and bridge were filmed on Elstree's Stage Five, which the studios had long been using as a storage shed. It didn't have the soundproofing of the other soundstages, in addition to being home to a number of pigeons, making conditions for the crew less than perfect.

As a means of cutting costs, an early design for two separate sets for both areas was abandoned. Instead they were combined, with Ackbar's command area on a mezzanine level overlooking the briefing room. A shot of rebels arriving in that briefing room was filmed first, using a handheld camera. "What we were striving for was reality," said director Richard Marquand, who used two cameras when shooting the rest of the scene—one to capture a wide shot of the briefing, while another picked out the reactions of the lead actors and background performers.

"The hardest thing was putting the actors in the right places," Marquand added. "It was difficult to get them to look casual. We wanted to make them look as though they were just a bunch of people in a World War II movie, and it took a while to get that."

01 Admiral Ackbar takes command of *Home One* prior to the Battle of Endor. (Previous spread)

02 The rebels amass for a crucial briefing aboard *Home One*. (Previous spread)

03 Mon Mothma and Ackbar brief the rebels. Original production art by Ralph McQuarrie.

04 The rebel fleet heads to Endor.

05 An early exploration of a rebel war room. Art by Norman Reynolds.

05

ENDOR

The verdant woodland glades of a privately owned area of redwood forest in Northern California played host to Ewoks, stormtroopers, and a squad of rebel commandos as the filming location for the Forest Moon of Endor, in the final act of *Return of the Jedi*. With exterior and interior sets at London's Elstree Studios, and effects shots created at Industrial Light & Magic, Endor was to become one of the most memorable planets in *Star Wars*.

The location selected for the live-action scenes was an area of forest owned by the Miller-Rellim Redwood Company, around 15 minutes from Crescent City, which was discovered by production coordinator Miki Herman during a recce for the movie. The 40-acre site offered numerous advantages to the production crew, not least that it offered a level and easily accessible setting, and that they could film whatever they needed to, without restriction—useful for the type of scenes they would be shooting.

"George [Lucas] and Norman [Reynolds] would much rather have photographed in a nature reserve or a National Park," admitted *Jedi* co-producer Jim Bloom. "But I knew from the very beginning that was unlikely: We were going in to shoot a battle sequence, with large explosions, troops running about, and Imperial walkers crashing through."

Different areas of the site were given names during principal photography, such as Spaghetti Stump, Norman's Log, Heart-Shaped Tree, and Bunker Hill, where the Imperial bunker was constructed, midway up an incline. Given that the redwood forests were prone to periods of

inclement weather, the bunker had been built to resist the elements. "It rained for months up there prior to shooting and we just couldn't let it rain through," recalled Howard Kazanjian.

The full-sized scout walker prop was assembled at Bunker Hill, while the Ewok's raised walkways and rope bridge occupied other areas of the site. Ewok warrior Paploo was able to steal a speeder bike thanks to it being attached to a dolly and track and pulled out of shot by the crew.

Peter Mayhew was told not to wander off alone while wearing his Chewbacca costume, in case he was mistaken for the legendary Big Foot. ☻

01

04

FOREST L. Burner

05

FOREST STEVE -LOCKETT

01 An Imperial walker on patrol. (Previous spread)

02 The cast pose on location. (Previous spread)

03 Luke Skywalker is brought to Darth Vader. Original production art by Ralph McQuarrie.

04 A swatch showing the pallette for the rebels Endor uniforms.

05 Two continuity Polarioids taken of rebel troopers on location. Unlisted on any call sheets, these rebels were likely locals recruited for the shoot.

06/07/08 Luke, Han, and Leia in Endor attire.

06   07   08

SPEEDER BIKE CHASE

Among the many thrilling sequences in *Return of the Jedi*, the speeder bike chase through the forest landscape of Endor was a stand out. Filmed with a combination of miniatures, life-sized props, live-action location footage, and actors against blue screens, the chase provided theater audiences with three minutes of adrenaline-pumping action, but took far longer to create.

 J oe Johnston, Ralph McQaurrie, and Nilo Rodis-Jamero generated more than 200 concept drawings for the speeder bikes before Johnston switched to kitbashing to refine their ideas into a finished design. Four full-sized props were built by the art department at Elstree studios, and it fell to ILM modelshop staff Ira Keeler, Mike Fulmer, and Mike Cochrane to build the miniature versions required for visual effects. With no blueprints available, the modelmakers crafted scaled down miniatures using measurements from one of the full-sized props.

Nilo Rodis-Jamero also defined the look of the Imperial scout trooper in a series of concept sketches, which were then translated into physical form by Keeler. The helmet was cast out of ABS plastic so it could be lightweight. Keeler devised the detailing for the helmet, such as the breathing filter. "That was made from a piece of plastic from a model kit, a motorcycle head fin, and the nozzle of a kitchen faucet," the modelmaker said.

Dennis Muren, Ken Ralston, and Richard Edlund at ILM started exploring ideas for how to complete the forest chase. Edlund mused, "We were worried about how we were going to shoot the backgrounds. There was talk about flying a camera on long cables through the forest but then how do you get rid of the cables?"

The sequence itself was previsualized by Muren and Ralston, who shot videomatics to compose the visual effects elements of the chase using a model landscape made of carboard tubes painted brown to represent trees, with off-the-shelf Kenner *Star Wars* action figures riding basic models of the speeder bikes.

As the deadline fast approached Edlund hit upon the solution to shoot the background plates live-action forest backgrounds were shot using a Steadicam rig with a camera shooting at a low frame rate mounted to it. Garrett Brown, the inventor of the Steadicam, was hired to shoot the footage at a redwood forest location near Crescent City, walking slowly through the landscape as directed by Muren. When processed and run at normal speed, the footage gave the effect of moving through the trees at approximately 120 mph.

02

03

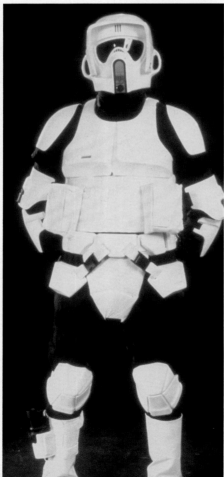

01 A production image
of a scout trooper in
front of the Imperial
bunker. (Previous
spread)

02 The EC-17
blaster as used
by the scout troopers.

03 A specialized
stormtrooper variant,
the scout troopers
generally took part in
reconnaissance
missions.

04 The puppet speeder
bike model is
manipulated by (left)
Bobby Finley and (right)
Phil Tippett.
in order to show the
maneuverability of
these Imperial vehicles.

05

06

08

"Dennis and Garrett shot the background plates following a string on the ground as a patern," Edlund said. "Later if the camera moved off the string for one frame, we could optically adjust that frame. We ended up going through all that footage, fixing, and vaseline-ing it."

Once the backgrounds were achieved, the team employed Go-Motion puppet animation to incorporate the characters into the shots. First employed to make the tauntans gallop through the icy terrain of Hoth in *The Empire Strikes Back*, the technique used stop motion puppets with certain motorized joints that moved just slightly as the camera shot a single frame. In the final shot, this movement gave the illusion of motion blur rather than strobing, mime-like look of some stop-motion. For most of the shots, Luke, Leia and the speeder bike pilots were scale puppets shot against a bluescreen with rods protruding from their backs and heads. The puppets were shot at a regular speed as the rods were slowly pulled to create the sense of natural movement.

Actors Mark Hamill and Carrie Fisher were then filmed against a blue screen astride full size speeder bike props at ILM in order to achieve closeup shots of Luke and Leia as they tear through the forest. ☮

05 Luke prepares to take down an incoming speeder bike.

06 Mark Hamill and Carrie Fisher film their close-ups on the blue screen set.

07 Dramatic production art by Ralph MacQuarrie captures the high-veolcity chase through the trees.

08 McQuarrie's early exploration of the look of the speeder bikes.

EWOKS

Native inhabitants of the Forest Moon of Endor, the Ewoks became the unlikely heroes of *Return of the Jedi*. Short in stature and with only wood and stone weapons to defend themselves, they were the antithesis of the Empire, which had all the technology of a galaxy at its disposal. For George Lucas, that was the whole point.

 "Originally, I started writing *Star Wars* because I couldn't get *Apocalypse Now* (1979) off the ground," Lucas said. "[That] was about this totally insane, giant technological society that was fighting these poor little people. They have little sticks and things, and yet they completely cow this technological power, because the technological power didn't believe they were any threat. They were just a bunch of peasants. The main theme of [*Jedi*] was that the Imperial Empire would be overrun by humanity in the form of these cute little teddy bears."

Lucas had explored the idea in some of his original outlines for *A New Hope*, in which Wookiees had played the role of a primitive society defeating an advanced foe. Because Chewbacca had become a character with technological understanding in that movie, the filmmaker had to think up a new species for the third installment. "I thought, I can't make them Wookiees, so I'll make them *short* Wookiees, and give them short hair and a different society, and make them really primitive, the way it was intended," Lucas has said.

Described by Lucas to Joe Johnston as "little furry guys" carrying spears in the woods, the art department produced hundreds of sketches to that brief. "A lot of them were troll-like, or gnomes, and all kinds of little things," Johnston recalled. "George came in and said, 'This isn't working. Let's make them cuter.'"

After further concepts (with cute furry ears and animal skin accessories) were approved by Lucas, it was time to begin building the Ewok costumes. Stuart Freeborn was tasked with crafting the creature's heads, while the wardrobe team under Janet Tebrooke worked on the bodies. Stalwart *Star Wars* performers Kenny Baker and Jack Purvis arrived at Elstree Studios to have body casts taken of them that would form the basis for the Ewok costume molds.

01

01 Warwick Davis and his sister, Kim, take a break.

02 Warwick Davis in full costume as Ewok warrior, Wicket W. Warrick.

03

Test footage of actors wearing prototype Ewok costumes was shot in Black Park, close to Pinewood Studios near London—a location that would years later appear briefly as Endor in *Star Wars: The Rise of Skywalker* (2019).

"The Ewoks were shot on a long lens running through the undergrowth, running, turning, dancing, sitting, and standing up, to see if there were any costume problems, which there were," director Marquand acknowledged. "Their eyes misted up instantly. So Stuart and his gang got down to solving that problem, which was to pinch little holes all the way around to let the heat out. We also realized that we had to give them more articulation."

Along with these structural fixes, wardrobe mistress Janet Tebrooke further enhanced the costumes with "feathers, old bones, sticks, acorns, and bits of dead birds," that she thought an Ewok might find useful.

The Ewok village set was constructed at Elstree Studios in England. Its platforms and linking rope bridges were raised above the studio floor by a few meters to give the impression that the Ewoks had built their homes high in the treetops. A painted cyclorama backdrop featuring a forest background and sky was hung behind the wooden huts and prop tree trunks, further adding to the impression of great height.

04

03 Although Kenny Baker is better known for his role as R2-D2, he also played the Ewok scout, Paploo.

04 A playful sketch by Joe Johnston.

05 Teebo, as played by *Star Wars* veteran Jack Purvis, who had previously appeared as a Jawa and an Ugnaught.

08

09

Around 120 people applied for roles after Lucasfilm made a public appeal for actors of short stature to get in touch. One of those was an 11-year old *Star Wars* fan named Warwick Davis, who had heard of the casting call from his grandmother. By this time, the production had cast most of the performers it needed, but they were still looking for people to play younger Ewoks.

"My mom called the studio. I think she told them that I loved *Star Wars*, but she [also] said that I was young," Davis recalled. "That's how I managed to get a meeting. So I took the day off school and went up to Elstree Studios in London. All I did was show a lot of enthusiasm and had my measurements taken, and that was it; there was no audition or anything like that. For Wicket it was down to my enthusiasm. That's what got me in the door. I don't think anybody on the movie was quite as excited as I was. Being an 11-year-old on a *Star Wars* film, there was no stopping me."

"The challenge of creating a likable character out of a kid in a bear suit was difficult," Lucas observed. "You're always asking yourself how far can you go, so I was fortunate to find Warwick, who was so expressive in his suit and had such personality in the way he walked and in the way he carried himself. He was one-hundred percent into the character."

06 Actor Mike Edmonds, who also operated Jabba the Hutt's tail, plays the Ewok shaman, Logray.

07 The rebels find themselves at the wrong end of the Ewoks' spears.

08 Makeup artist Kay Freeborn creates an Ewok mask.

09 The youngest members of the tribe listen to C-3PO's tale.

10 R2-D2 and
Wicket bond at
Bright Tree Village.

11 A matte painting
depicting the Bright
Tree Village by artist
Mike Pangrazio. Live
action is added to the
blacked-out parts of
the image to create
the final shot.

12 An Ewok carries
its young. Art by
Joe Johnston.

13 Carrie Fisher and
Warwick Davis bonded
on location with the
actress feeding the
young actor milk and
cookies between takes.

14 Tribal elders Logray
and Chief Chirpa, played
by Jane Busby.

15 Imperial scout
trooper's equipment
is repurposed by an Ewok
warrior. Art by Joe
Johnston.

12

15

Choreographer Gillian Gregory was engaged to give movement classes to the actors and extras who would be playing the forest dwellers. Marquand asked Gregory to use mirrors during the training sessions, so that the performers would better understand how their movements translated through the hefty costumes. The director also came up with a specific body language for the Ewoks, a range of gestures that would lend the creatures a common physical language.

The battle scenes involving Ewoks were filmed in the U.S.A., during principal photography for the exterior Endor scenes in an area of woodland owned by the Miller-Rellim Redwood Company. But the location shoot required an entirely different set of Ewok performers, in addition to Davis, Baker, and Purvis.

"These were now American Ewoks," explained Marquand. "So we had a whole new training program and a whole new lot of costumes made. They used to go on walks and rambles and hikes and runs to get up their strength. By the time they reached me, they were very much fitter and more energetic than they had been when they'd been cast."

"It was very difficult to get the Ewoks to really seem threatening," Lucas later admitted. "They're designed to be cute and fuzzy, virtual teddy bears; but they're also the ones who save the day, so they had to have this dual capacity. I knew the older kids would have trouble buying into this idea, but we decided to do it anyway." ☻

THE FIGHT ON THE FOREST MOON

The climactic finale of *Return of the Jedi* took place on three fronts. Luke Skywalker faced off against Darth Vader and the Emperor on the second Death Star, while a grand space battle took place in the shadow of the space station. The third front was the culmination of an ambition George Lucas had harbored since beginning his *Star Wars* odyssey: a massive ground battle where a primitive species would confront and overcome the technological might of the Empire.

F or the *Jedi* production crew, however, logistics was the biggest obstacle they had to overcome. Having secured their preferred filming location, and dressed the area with Imperial equipment and extra vines and greenery, it was time to shoot scene 115—the battle of Lucas' dreams. In all, the Empire would be represented by 130 extras dressed as Imperial stormtroopers, officers, guards, and pilots. They would be pitched against 40 Ewoks and a handful of rebel troops. The scene would be shot using five cameras to ensure full coverage of the battlefield. Another film crew was also on set to document the shoot.

"It was mayhem, chaos, because of the very nature of the shooting," remembered Marquand. "Shooting in the forest meant that it was very much harder to have crowd control. You'd say to the Ewok extras, 'Run, disappear, hide!' But then you'd find that they were lost; you don't know where they've gone and it's difficult to get them to come back again."

First assistant director David Tomblin, Marquand, and Lucas combined forces to wrangle their army of cast members, ensuring the primary battlefield action was successfully captured on film. However, minor skirmishes and action vignettes still had to be shot in other parts of the woodland location, and filming continued for several weeks after the main unit had wrapped. Second unit camera crews filmed sequences of Ewoks fighting stormtroopers with reference to detailed storyboards, although they were given "freedom to improvise on a theme," according to Tomblin.

"The camera crews were marvelously cooperative," he said. "I'd have a briefing every morning and give each of them their workload. We could stretch our cameras to four units at four different locations, as long as they stayed within commuting distance."

Another lengthy battle was fought by ILM, who had an unprecedented number of visual effects shots to complete, including around 50 featuring AT-ST walkers.

Several AT-STs were constructed. A 16-inch model built around an aluminum and steel armature would be used for stop-motion animation, and a four-foot version was built for shots where the vehicle needed to be "destroyed." Several heads were made for this model, using materials such as aluminum-filled epoxy and brittle wax—whatever was best suited to effectively portray the type of destruction that would be visited upon it. A head made from .05-inch nickel was specifically built for the scene a walker's head was smashed between two logs in an Ewok trap.

02

03

04

01 Chewbacca
commendeers an AT-ST.
(Previous spread)

02 The rebels fight to
gain accces to the
Imperial bunker.

03 The bunker is
built on location in
the redwood forest.

04 A model AT-ST
is constructed.

05 Stormtroopers
find themselves
under attack from
the vicious Ewoks.

06

06 The Ewoks join the
fight! Production art
by Ralph McQuarrie.

07 Director Richard
Marquand (holding the
megaphone) directs
Kenny Baker as Paploo
hijacks a speeder bike.

Dennis Muren utilized his
Go-Motion technique to film
the AT-ST in action, and shots
were filmed on a model set of
the Endor forest placed in the
ILM building's backlot, to make
use of natural sunlight.

"The most difficult shot
was with the trees when the
walker trips on them," Phil
Tippett confirmed.

"That was a difficult and
time-consuming shot, right
from the start," agreed Muren.

"The logs would come
down too fast—like a couple

of pencils rolling down—as
opposed to massive logs falling
and hitting each other, bouncing
and twisting," said Peterson.
The sequence was filmed at high
speed, which gave the tumbling
logs the impression weight when
the film was projected at 24fps.

ILM also had to create
believable forest miniatures
that would fit seamlessly with
the location footage. Lorne
Peterson supervised a team
of modelmakers tasked with
building a forest of redwood
trees at two different scales, with

trunks ranging from half an inch
to 16 inches in diameter. Sprigs
of juniper, small branches, leaves,
and even dried tumbleweed were
employed to add realism to the
miniature sets.

"We tried making them out
of a variety of things, including
small redwood trees," said
Peterson. To enable them to
create the number of trees
required, Barbara Gallucci
sculpted trunks with different
diameters, which were then
molded and cast using flexible
and rigid urethane.

09

The turning point in the ground battle came when the rebels finally destroyed the shield generator protecting the Death Star. Dennis Muren used a variation on a decades old effects technique, capturing the entire scene in-camera. A model of the radar dish was placed between a painted backdrop and a foreground of trees painted onto a glass plate. A scrim was hung between the glass and the model, lit to emulate the planet's atmosphere thereby suggesting the dish was some distance away. The scene was then shot with a high-speed camera, shooting at 300fps.

"For the dish itself, I didn't want a prefabricated look, so Lorne Peterson made it the way a real thing would be built, with struts and fabric materials," explained Muren. He didn't want the model to visibly lift off the ground when it exploded. "It blew up and did all the things a big model is supposed to do—in one take. It was real quick. From concept to completed shot took about three or four days."

08

08 Han, Leia, and Chewie storm the Imperial bunker.

09 Han leads the rebels on the ground against the Imperial troops.

10

11

10 A behind-the-scenes shot of an Ewok hang glider in action!

11 A behind-the-scenes shot of stormtrooper stunt performer (second from left) Sandy Gross, pictured here taking a break on location with (from left) Mike Cassidy, Julius Le Flore, and dresser Barbara Affonso, shows that the Imperial forces are not limited to just men.

12 The Ewoks use primitive weapons to beat the more technologically advanced stormtroopers.

13 R2-D2 takes a hit.

12

15

14 The rebels
surrounded by
stormtroopers.

15 Han attempts to
gain entry into the
bunker while Leia
defends their position.

16 Han brandishes his
heavy blaster pistol.

The back entrance to the bunker was built in the redwood forest location. An economic slump in the area meant that there were at local workers happy to clear the area.

Production designer Norman Reynolds team imported some "old-man's beard," the same vines that appear as set dressing on Dagobah in *The Empire Strikes Back* and The Temple of the Chachapoyan Warriors in *Raiders of the Lost Ark*.

The bunker entrance, located at Bunker Hill, was built so that people could walk in and down a small flight of steps. The lights and doors were operational and the structure was constructed to resist the elements including the potentially devastating impact of impact from a falling branch.

When Han's team finally gain access to the bunker an extended shoot out was filmed but discarded in postproduction. Solo's confrontation with the Imperial who calls Han "rebel scum" took a day and a half of continuous filming, with Ford lightening the mood by playfully slapping the actor, Barrie Holland, on the face.

For the shot of the Imperial officer who gets knocked off of his feet when Han Solo knocks him over a railing, *Star Wars'* sound designer, Ben Burtt donned a uniform and took on the role at the request of George Lucas. The officer's death cry was Burtt himself, imitating the famous "Wilhelm" Scream that recurs across the franchise.

During the skirmish, Han and Leia repeat their, "I love you," "I know" exchange from *The Empire Strikes Back*, but this time with the lines switched over. As Chewbacca and his Ewok companions swing onto the scout walker, the Wookiee emits a Tarzan yell as popularized in the movies by Johnny Weissmuller.

When shooting concluded the set was dismantled in a matter of hours and the hole in which the bunker was positioned was filled in. From the day the unit arrived to film the sequences it never rained again for the whole duration of the shoot. ☮

THE BATTLE OF ENDOR

The climactic space battle of *A New Hope* had wowed theater audiences in 1977 with it's thrilling dogfights and Luke Skywalker's tense trench run targeting the Death Star's thermal exhaust port. With a second Death Star to destroy in *Return of the Jedi*, George Lucas set ILM the task of creating an even more spectacular battle.

Perhaps the biggest challenge the *Return of the Jedi* crew faced was topping what had gone before.

"The first *Star Wars* movie was really unique. *The Empire Strikes Back* had to be technically and aesthetically advanced from that, and *Jedi* has to outdo *Empire*," said Joe Johnston at the prospect. "I think the public has grown to expect that they are not going to see the same old thing. They want to see something better."

"Every film George does has to be bigger than the last," said Ken Ralston, visual effects supervisor on *Jedi*. That was reflected in the number of ILM staff who would be working on the film, which amounted to 140 model makers, camera operators, matte artists, animators, compositors, and other specialties. The total cost projection for the movie's effects budget was estimated at

$9,475,230, (around a million dollars less than *Empire's* effects budget, adjusted for inflation). Each shot would therefore cost, on average, $22K. The rebel attack alone would consist of 102 shots, each of which would involve multiple elements that all had to be brought together.

"When we started [on *Return of the Jedi*] we said 'Ok, we're going to do it the way we always wanted to do it. We've got the money, we're got the knowledge—this is it.'" George Lucas said.

Different aspects of the battle were split between two of the movie's visual effects supervisors. Ralston was responsible for the bulk of the space combat shots, while Richard Edland looked after the chase through the Death Star's tunnels and its vast reactor chamber.

Given the sheer number of individual elements required for the ambitious space battle, ILM was fortunate to have advanced

several technologies thanks to the many film projects it had been involved with since *The Empire Strikes Back*. The company also had a new motion-control tracking camera called the VistaCruiser, which had been conceived as the next generation of the Dykstraflex camera, built for *A New Hope*. The VistaCruiser would be used for many of the Death Star surface shots, and the Dykstraflex was also pressed back into service for the movie. In addition, ILM had built an extremely malleable setup called the G-9 Rama, a boom-mounted, computer-controlled camera that could tilt through 135 degrees and move along a track.

As had been done for *A New Hope*, footage of World War II aerial combat had been compiled as a previsualization tool to help develop starship movement and dynamics. The sequence was also extensively storyboarded and videomatics filmed to further refine shots.

01 Storyboard art showing a TIE interceptor following the *Millennium Falcon* into the Death Star.

02

02 The rebel fleet under attack!
Original production art by Ralph McQuarrie.

03

03 The rebel fleet battles the might of the Empire.

04 In this storyboard art B-wings and TIE bombers fly through the Death Star superstructure. Neither ship makes the journey in the final cut.

"We're finding that the choreography is very important," said Ken Ralston. "There's a lot going on. Most of the shots are quite short and some of them are so busy—ships flying around and explosions all over the place—that we'll be in dailies and the shot'll come and go and we'll still be sitting there wondering what the hell it was. All you can see is movement."

The pressure to complete the shots required mounted. A shot that might last a second or two on screen encorporating two dozen spaceships could use as many as 57 seperate elements which meant 57 pieces of film,

56 for the ships and one for the starfield background. George Lucas would then approve every individual element before giving final sign off. The crew would work round the clock, wih a nightshift keeping the assembly line of shots moving forwards. The team called themselves "Optical Dogs" after a sequence in the 1982 film *Poltergeist* in which a dog walked into frame and looked up at actress JoBeth Williams who was on the ceiling. To lighten the mood amonst the crew, the team would add the dog into *Return of the Jedi*'s various set pieces.

One of the challenges faced

by the team was to make sure that the sharp lens used by the department wasn't too sharp. Ken Ralston explained, "If the image is too clear, too sharp, it shows all the unwanted details."

This was not the only problem that befell the visual effects team. Up to 100 shots were changed when George Lucas made the descision to restructure the film. Dubbed "Black Friday" after the stock market crash, months of work was undone. One sequence had $250,000 worth of work on it. The crew had little choice but to accept the change of direction and move on.

05

Lending a human perspective to the space battle, footage of pilots in fighter cockpits was shot with actors recounting lines of dialogue fed to them through an earpiece.

Directing the attack from the cockpit of the *Millennium Falcon*, Lando Calrissian (Billy Dee Williams) had been given more dialogue during a script rewrite just a few weeks ahead of production. Richard Marquand elected to shoot Calrissian's lines in one long take.

"Poor Billy was very confused," the director admitted. "I mean, it's the worst thing in the world to sit in this seat and there's nothing there, but in front of you is a barrage of cameras and me, yelling and screaming, and machines going and lights crossing backward and forward. If you can remember your lines, you're a genius, let alone give a performance."

05 Nein Nunb and Lando Calrissian pilot the *Falcon*.

The puppeteer behind Admiral Ackbar was Tim Rose, who had operated Salacious B. Crumb during the scenes at Jabba's palace. The Mon Calamari officer was described in an early draft of the script as "pale blue, non-human." However, when director Richard Marquand was taking part in a concept approval session, he was taken by the maquette of what he described as "the most delicious, wonderful creature out of the whole lot, this great, big wonderful Calamari man with a red face and eyes on the side."

"With Admiral Ackbar, I asked George which eye I should keep on the camera, beacuse no matter what I did with him, he was always going to look shifty because he was wall-eyed. I told George that two things I learned from the *Muppets* were the importance of crisp mouth movement and eye focus, so Ackbar wasn't going to look like the strong leader we wanted him to be. I stuck my hand up his faux head and showed George what I meant. I later made a special pair of eyes for Ackbar so that when he looked at someone he focussed on them. That gave him empathy and that's how the close-up shots of him were shot."

Actor Dermot Crowley, who played General Madine was unexpectedly presented with a beard on his first day of shooting. The reasoning for this was that the team at Kenner, the company that manufactured the successful line of *Star Wars* action figures, had begun preproduction and the toy had a beard.

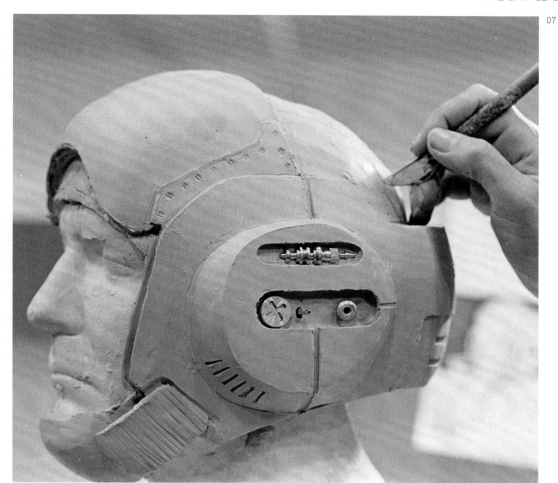

06 Admiral Ackbar leads the rebel fleet. Ackbar is puppeteered by Tim Rose who also operated Salacious B. Crumb.

07 An A-wing pilot helmet is carefully sculpted based on Nilo Rodis-Jamero's sketches (below).

08 The *Falcon* leads two X-wing fighters inside the second Death Star. (Following spread)

09 Ralph McQuarrie's original production painting sees the *Millennium Falcon* and *Red Two* fire upon the second Death Star's reactor core.

10 The *Falcon* makes a daring escape.

The ILM model shop was not only busy building starfighters, it also had to construct the intricate infrastructure of the Death Star, through which the *Millennium Falcon* would fly to reach the battle station's reactor core.

"Building the tunnels meant creating a series of trenches and tunnel sections that would be over 360 feet long," said ILM modelshop supervisor Steve Gawley. "We used several sizes of tubes because we wanted to create three distinct tunnel types, each 72 feet long. The walls were made of mirrored Plexiglas and each foot-long section of the ceiling came off for camera access." The model sets eventually used almost six miles of cardboard tubes from carpet rolls, and up to three miles of sprinkler pipe. ☺

THE FINAL DUEL

The duel between Luke Skywalker and Darth Vader in *Return of the Jedi* was far more than a straightforward rematch between the hero and villain. In *The Empire Strikes Back*, Luke's inexperience had seen him overwhelmed by Vader during a battle he'd barely survived. By *Jedi*, however, Skywalker's training was complete, and he possessed all the skills he needed to at least match his father. Perhaps even defeat him. Yet both were facing a far more powerful and cunning foe—the Emperor himself.

The trap that the Emperor had set for the rebel fleet was not the sole reason behind his presence on the second Death Star. His true plan was to use the plight of Skywalker's friends to turn the young Jedi to the dark side and take the place of Darth Vader.

"The temptations facing Luke are so enormous that you cannot actually see how it's possible to solve them and

save him. It's such a complex situation," Richard Marquand said. "George and I had long conversations about the Emperor and the final act of the movie and how the Emperor would turn the tables on Luke. And George went away writing and he came up with the most terrible double-cross."

"The Emperor is playing the two against each other to see which one wins," George Lucas explained. "[He wants] Luke to turn to the dark side and become his apprentice by killing Vader.

Vader doesn't quite understand that he's on the chopping block, until he gets into that fight. He thinks that his job is to kill the kid, but of course he can't really kill [Luke], and the Emperor knows that he can't."

The Emperor's throne room set, where the scenes between the Galactic despot, Vader, and Skywalker took place, was built on Stage 4 at Elstree, and like the scenes set in Jabba the Hutt's Tatooine equivalent, Marquand opted to shoot the sequence in chronological order.

01 The Emperor's guards flank Vader and his prisoner.

02 Darth Vader and Luke Skywalker head toward a confrontation with the Emperor.

03 Richard Marquand
directs Ian McDiarmid
and Mark Hamill.

04 Luke reacts to the Emperor's taunts.

05 Darth Vader defends his Emperor as Luke fights back.

Unlike the spectacular fight seen in *Empire,* the *Jedi* duel was less "action fireworks as much as two characters confronting each other," according to actor Mark Hamill.

Hamill had been in training with fight coordinator Peter Diamond and stuntman Bob Anderson (who donned the Darth Vader costume for the duel) for four weeks prior to shooting the sequence. With more than 275 movies under his belt, Diamond was an expert in multiple forms of martial arts and swordplay—knowledge he employed in arranging the fight and fine-tuning the skills of the actors who performed it. Every step of the fight was plotted like a ballet, with Diamond choreographing each footfall.

"I have to think about how it's going to look photographically," Diamond explained. "And an actor's interpretation of character has to come into it. Errol Flynn couldn't fence, but he knew photographically what looked good on the screen. Mark has now got a Flynn-quality about him. He's a very good swordsman now."

"There was a shot in which my lightsaber had to jump into my hand," Hamill recalled. "We shot it backward: I had to enter the shot as though I was exiting it with my final mood intact. Then I had to make an abrupt move into calmness, put my hand up, and throw my sword away. It was very difficult to coordinate, very much like mime."

There were three dramatic stages to the confrontation that represented Luke's personal conflict. First, succumbing to the Emperor's encouragement, he gave in to temptation and attempted to slay the Emperor. Vader defended his master and the two fought until the second stage of the fight, where Luke withdrew, hiding in the shadows. Vader's threat to turn Leia to the dark side enraged Luke, who beats Vader to the ground, repeatedly bringing his lightsaber

06 Stunt performer Bob Anderson, doubling as Darth Vader, and Mark Hamill clash lightsabers in this behind-the-scenes shot. (Previous spread)

07 Luke tries to win Vader over from the dark side.

08 The Emperor unleashes his fury on Luke.

down until Vader's cybernetic right hand breaks off.

"During the final confrontation, when Luke has Vader on the ground, the red lights of the elevator were design elements but were also there specifically," Lucas later revealed. "The color goes symbolically into the blood of the father and son, and a move toward hell—because this is where Luke is either going to go to hell or not."

Recognizing the dark path he was about to take, Luke Skywalker chose to discard his lightsaber and reaffirm his place as a Jedi, much to the Emperor's disgust. The lightning bolts the Emperor unleashed, which were added during post production, were enough to finally cause Darth Vader to turn on his master to save his son.

"I had to come back to do some reshooting on my 'death.' I was on a harness and had to be lifted up by Darth Vader," McDiarmid recollected. Doing the lifting was Darth Vader actor David Prowse, although the original plan had been for stuntman Bob Anderson to do the deed.

"Their idea was to attach wires to the Emperor and have [Bob] Anderson lift him up

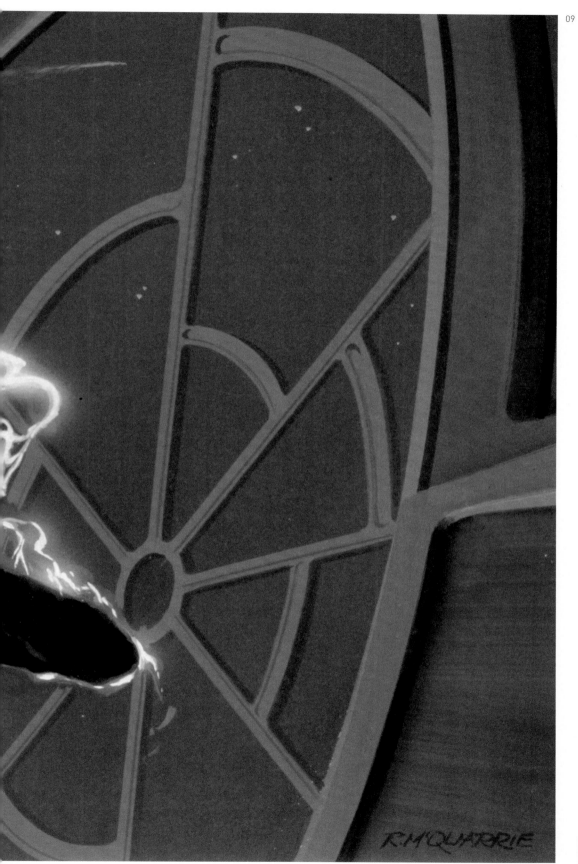

09 The Emperor strikes back! Production art by Ralph McQuarrie.

while somebody pulled on the wires. They tried it that way for two days, but it wouldn't work. Anderson is nearly 60 and couldn't lift the Emperor," explained Prowse. "I suggested that I could do it easily."

Prowse, who was suffering from a knee injury, was eventually asked to perform the stunt. "I was on crutches, but I knew I could still do the shot," the former weightlifter said. "I simply picked the Emperor

up, lifted him above my head, and threw him off the balcony. I did it in one take."

The Emperor's defeat at the cost of his Vader's life is followed by the crucial scene in which Luke removes his father's mask to reveal the man, Anakin Skywalker, beneath. Referred to as "The Man" on call sheets as a security measure, veteran actor Sebastian Shaw took the role of Luke's father.

Richard Marquand had originally wanted a well-known English theatrical actor to play Anakin before George Lucas dissuaded him believing that the actor should not be a household name.

"They decided they needed a very experienced actor to play that very difficult scene," Sebastian Shaw said. "They didn't tell me what I was going to have to do, because they were being so careful."☙

10 A behind-the-scenes shot as Vader turns on his master to protect Luke.

11 Actor Sebastian Shaw played Anakin Skywalker beneath the mask. Shaw's eyebrows would later be digitally removed in keeping with the former Jedi's injuries.

POST-PRODUCTION

With filming completed on *Return of the Jedi*, the movie was
ready to be shaped during the post-production process.

 was not until
principal
photography
had been
completed on
*Return of the
Jedi* that George Lucas decided
to include the funeral scene.
Lucas reasoned that because
Anakin's death scene ended
with the character in Luke's
arms, the audience might
construe that the character
was not dead and could return.

Another last minute shot
came when Dennis Muren
completed the X-wing fly past
as fireworks light up the sky
over Endor. The pyrotechnics

were shot in slow motion and
the footage was shown upside
down so that the streamers went
upwards in an offbeat way. Ken
Ralston shot the X-wings for
the sequence using an X-wing
model kit that measured an inch
wide. He painted the engines
a fluorescent color and lit the
model to give the impression
that the engines were glowing.
The tilt upwards from live action
to the Endor night sky was
achieved with a matte painting
by Michael Pangrazio. The rain
that fell during the filming
of the funeral pyre sequence
created a smear of orange light
as the camera tilted which

helped blend the shots together.

Bluescreen filming was
required for the Ewok
celebration sequence as the
highly flammable costumes
were a fire risk.

With designs inspired by
Ralph MacQuarrie's paintings
for 1995's *The Illustrated Star
Wars Universe* book, the look
of Coruscant was sketched by
Lucasfilm's director of concept
design, Doug Chaing. George
Lucas wanted the cityscape to
be sleek, a city of old and new
architecture, art deco and art
modern. Chaing recalls, "It
was like taking Manhatten and
scaling it way, way up."

01

01 Celebration on the streets of Coruscant as the galaxy cheers the fall of the Empire.

02 An eleventh hour inclusion, Anakin's funeral pyre was constructed and filmed at Skywalker Ranch.

03 The Ewoks lead the revelry as the rebels commemorate their victory.

John Williams provided a lush score that expanded on his themes for the first two movies. During the scoring sessions, Ian McDiarmid noticed a sequence that just featured the score and no dialogue. Remarking to George Lucas that it reminded him of a silent movie, Lucas responded that in many ways it is. The dialogue is not of paramount importance. For the first time ever a lightsaber duel was scored. Ben Burtt, whose sound design previously led in these sequences said that, "The music was more important in delivering the emotional satisfaction of the moment than the sound effects. John wrote a terrific cue for the choir." The shot of Obi-Wan Kenobi, Yoda, and Anakin Skywalker reunited as Force spirits was included by Lucas to give a sense of closure to Luke's relationship with his father.

The actor who played the unmasked Anakin, Sebastian Shaw, returned to the set to film the final scene, "George Lucas actually directed me. Alec Guinness wasn't there, it was all put together afterward. When we were filming the sequence, I didn't know why we were doing it.; I thought it was for publicity. George just said, "Look happy. Smile."

While the 1997 re-release of *Return of the Jedi* saw Anakin retain his original identity as Sebastian Shaw, the 2004 DVD release of the film made a key change. The original actor was replaced by Hayden Christensen, who took the role in the prequel films, in a shot taken during the production of the then upcoming *Revenge of the Sith*.

04 A behind-the-scenes shot as Billy Dee Williams. Kenny Baker, Peter Mayhew, Harrison Ford, Carrie Fisher, Mark Hamill and Anthony Daniels pose on the Ewok village set.

04

05 The original Anakin
Skywalker, Sebastian
Shaw (above) was
replaced by Hayden
Christensen in the
2004 DVD release.

AFTERLIFE

The release of *Return of the Jedi* marked not only
the end of the original trilogy, but years of work by George Lucas and his team.

eleased on Wednesday, May 25, *Return of the Jedi* was met with fevered hype from audiences who had waited 3 years for resolution to the loose strands left by *The Empire Strikes Back*. Theaters scheduled back-to-back screenings to meet demand and there were reports of people skipping work to see the movie.

The film set a new single-day record, the largest opening-day gross ever, taking $6,219,629 from 1,002 screens, going on to take $30 million in it's opening weekend, overtaking the record set by *E.T. The Extra Terrestrial* (1982).

Tom Sherak, Fox's president of domestic distribution and marketing, commented that, "you don't see anybody not smiling. I can't tell you how many kids I heard asking their parents if they can see the film again."

The movie enjoyed even more success all around the world as it broke box office records and played to packed houses throughout 1983.

Like the first two films in the saga, the release of *Return of the Jedi* was supported by various pieces of tie-in merchandise, including a novelization, a comic book adaptation, Topps trading cards, a soundtrack album, and, of course, new waves of Kenner action figures and vehicles adding to an already comprehensive range. Less than a month after the release of the film, over three million *Return of the Jedi* items had been sold, much to the delight of George Lucas who commented, "People tend to look at merchandising as an evil thing but a lot of fun things come out of it. It also pays for the overhead of the company and everybody's salary."

Although Lucas had expected the *Star Wars* saga to have faded from appeal after the release of *Return of the Jedi*, his foresight into audiences tastes had, for once, been wide of the mark. Although the flame had been kept alive in the mid-1980s by two made for television *Ewok* movies and a *Droids* and *Ewoks* animated series, it wasn't until 1997, when as part of the re-release of the original trilogy, *Return of the Jedi* returned to theaters as a new "Special Edition." The newly restored version presented a new take on the final scenes that were altered to show the galaxy in celebration after the Emperor and his evil Empire were brought down. The sequence showcased familair locales from previous films, Cloud City and Mos Eisley, before offering audiences their first glimpse of Coruscant, a world they would become much more familiar with over the forthcoming years as it took center stage in the *Star Wars* prequels....

Reflecting on the power of original trilogy years later, George Lucas said, "*Star Wars* is still as powerful as it ever was. There are still kids who are completely blown away by it. I get a lot of the joy back with kids. I realize what a powerful influence it's had on people, it's had a really powerful influence."

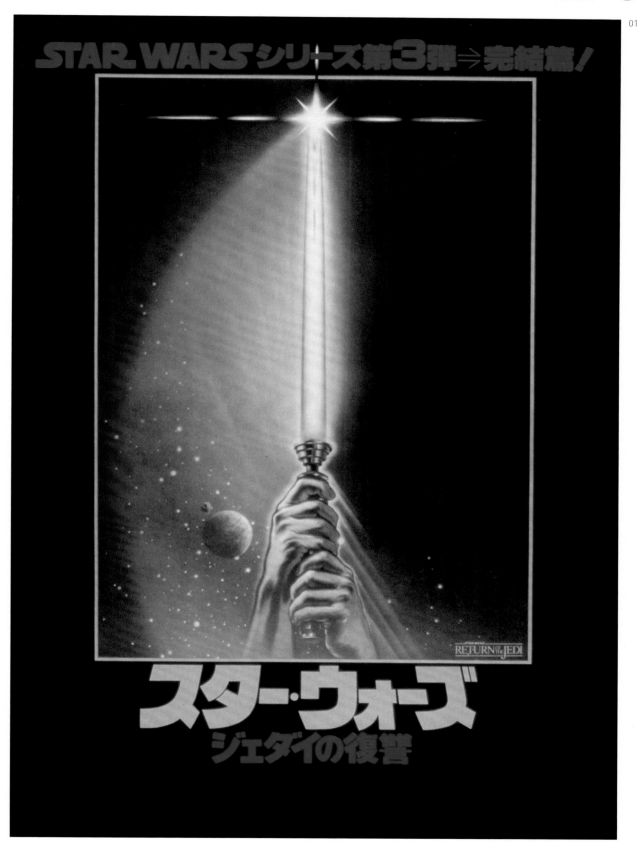

01 Japanese release poster, 1983. Art by Tim Reamer.

02

02 Polish theatrical one-sheet poster, 1984. Art by Witold Dybowski.

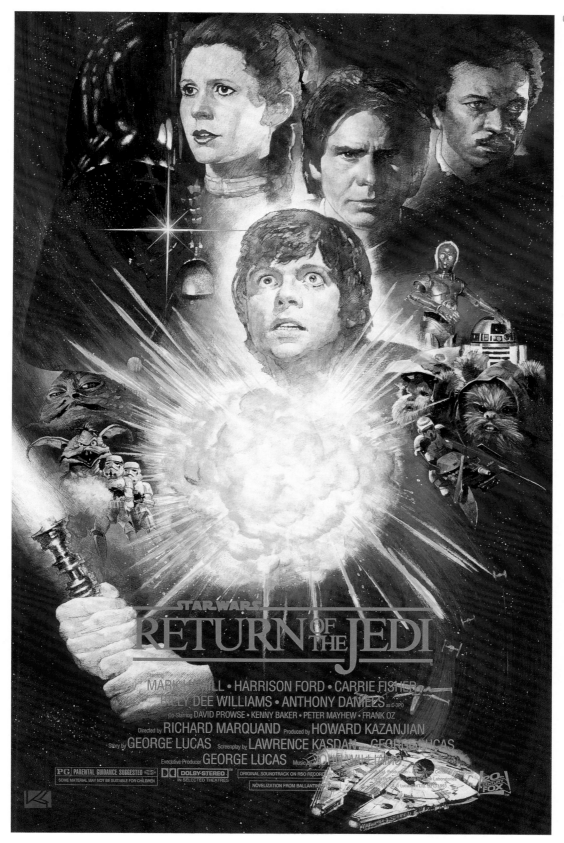

03 10th Anniversary poster 1993. Art by Kazuhiko Sano.

STAR WARS LIBRARY

STAR WARS: THE
MANDALORIAN
GUIDE TO SEASON ONE

STAR WARS: THE
MANDALORIAN
GUIDE TO SEASON TWO

STAR WARS INSIDER
PRESENTS THE MANDALORIAN
COLLECTION

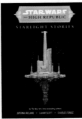

STAR WARS THE
HIGH REPUBLIC
STARLIGHT STORIES

STAR WARS THE
HIGH REPUBLIC
TALES OF ENLIGHTENMENT

STAR WARS:
RETURN OF THE JEDI
40TH ANNIVERSARY SPECIAL

- **ROGUE ONE: A STAR WARS STORY** THE OFFICIAL COLLECTOR'S EDITION
- **ROGUE ONE: A STAR WARS STORY** THE OFFICIAL MISSION DEBRIEF
- **STAR WARS: THE LAST JEDI** THE OFFICIAL COLLECTOR'S EDITION
- **STAR WARS: THE LAST JEDI** THE OFFICIAL MOVIE COMPANION
- **STAR WARS: THE LAST JEDI** THE ULTIMATE GUIDE
- **SOLO: A STAR WARS STORY** THE OFFICIAL COLLECTOR'S EDITION
- **SOLO: A STAR WARS STORY** THE ULTIMATE GUIDE
- **THE BEST OF STAR WARS INSIDER** VOLUME 1
- **THE BEST OF STAR WARS INSIDER** VOLUME 2

- **THE BEST OF STAR WARS INSIDER** VOLUME 3
- **THE BEST OF STAR WARS INSIDER** VOLUME 4
- **STAR WARS:** LORDS OF THE SITH
- **STAR WARS:** HEROES OF THE FORCE
- **STAR WARS:** ICONS OF THE GALAXY
- **STAR WARS:** THE SAGA BEGINS
- **STAR WARS** THE ORIGINAL TRILOGY
- **STAR WARS:** ROGUES, SCOUNDRELS AND BOUNTY HUNTERS
- **STAR WARS:** CREATURES, ALIENS, AND DROIDS
- **STAR WARS: THE RISE OF SKYWALKER** THE OFFICIAL COLLECTOR'S EDITION
- **STAR WARS: THE MANDALORIAN:** GUIDE TO SEASON ONE
- **STAR WARS: THE MANDALORIAN:** GUIDE TO SEASON TWO

- **STAR WARS: THE EMPIRE STRIKES BACK** THE 40TH ANNIVERSARY SPECIAL EDITION
- **STAR WARS: AGE OF RESISTANCE** THE OFFICIAL COLLECTORS' EDITION
- **STAR WARS: THE SKYWALKER SAGA** THE OFFICIAL COLLECTOR'S EDITION
- **STAR WARS INSIDER: FICTION COLLECTION** VOLUME 1
- **STAR WARS INSIDER: FICTION COLLECTION** VOLUME 2
- **STAR WARS INSIDER PRESENTS: MANDALORIAN SEASON 2** VOLUME 1
- **STAR WARS INSIDER PRESENTS: MANDALORIAN SEASON 2** VOLUME 2

MARVEL STUDIOS LIBRARY

MOVIE SPECIALS
- MARVEL STUDIOS' *SPIDER-MAN FAR FROM HOME*
- MARVEL STUDIOS' *ANT-MAN AND THE WASP*
- MARVEL STUDIOS' *AVENGERS: ENDGAME*
- MARVEL STUDIOS' *AVENGERS: INFINITY WAR*
- MARVEL STUDIOS' *BLACK PANTHER* (COMPANION)
- MARVEL STUDIOS' *BLACK WIDOW*
- MARVEL STUDIOS' *CAPTAIN MARVEL*
- MARVEL STUDIOS: THE FIRST TEN YEARS

- MARVEL STUDIOS' *THOR: RAGNAROK*
- MARVEL STUDIOS' *AVENGERS:*
  - AN INSIDER'S GUIDE TO THE *AVENGERS'* FILMS
- MARVEL STUDIOS' *WANDAVISION*
- MARVEL STUDIOS' *THE FALCON AND THE WINTER SOLDIER*
- MARVEL STUDIOS' *LOKI*
- MARVEL STUDIOS' *ETERNALS*
- MARVEL STUDIOS' *HAWKEYE*
- MARVEL STUDIOS' *SPIDER-MAN: NO WAY HOME*

MARVEL STUDIOS'
DOCTOR STRANGE IN THE
MULTIVERSE OF MADNESS
THE OFFICIAL MOVIE SPECIAL

MARVEL STUDIOS' PANTHER
WAKANDA FOREVER
THE OFFICIAL MOVIE SPECIAL

MARVEL STUDIOS' THOR:
LOVE AND THUNDER
THE OFFICIAL MOVIE SPECIAL

SPIDER-MAN: ACROSS THE
SPIDER-VERSE

MARVEL LEGACY LIBRARY

MARVEL'S CAPTAIN AMERICA:
THE FIRST 80 YEARS

MARVEL: THE FIRST
80 YEARS

MARVEL'S DEADPOOL:
THE FIRST 60 YEARS

MARVEL'S FANTASTIC FOUR:
THE FIRST 60 YEARS

MARVEL'S SPIDER-MAN:
THE FIRST 60 YEARS

MARVEL'S HULK:
THE FIRST 60 YEARS

MARVEL CLASSIC NOVELS
- WOLVERINE WEAPON X OMNIBUS
- SPIDER-MAN THE DARKEST HOURS OMNIBUS
- SPIDER-MAN THE VENOM FACTOR OMNIBUS
- X-MEN AND THE AVENGERS GAMMA QUEST OMNIBUS
- X-MEN MUTANT EMPIRE OMNIBUS

NOVELS
- MARVEL'S GUARDIANS OF THE GALAXY NO GUTS, NO GLORY
- SPIDER-MAN MILES MORALES WINGS OF FURY
- MORBIUS THE LIVING VAMPIRE: BLOOD TIES
- ANT-MAN NATURAL ENEMY
- AVENGERS EVERYBODY WANTS TO RULE THE WORLD

- AVENGERS INFINITY
- BLACK PANTHER WHO IS THE BLACK PANTHER?
- CAPTAIN AMERICA DARK DESIGNS
- CAPTAIN MARVEL LIBERATION RUN
- CIVIL WAR
- DEADPOOL PAWS
- SPIDER-MAN FOREVER YOUNG
- SPIDER-MAN KRAVEN'S LAST HUNT
- THANOS DEATH SENTENCE
- VENOM LETHAL PROTECTOR
- X-MEN DAYS OF FUTURE PAST
- X-MEN THE DARK PHOENIX SAGA
- SPIDER-MAN HOSTILE TAKEOVER

ART BOOKS
- *THE GUARDIANS OF THE GALAXY* THE ART OF THE GAME
- MARVEL'S *AVENGERS: BLACK PANTHER: WAR FOR WAKANDA* THE ART OF THE EXPANSION
- MARVEL'S *SPIDER-MAN MILES MORALES* THE ART OF THE GAME
- MARVEL'S *AVENGERS* THE ART OF THE GAME
- MARVEL'S *SPIDER-MAN* THE ART OF THE GAME
- MARVEL *CONTEST OF CHAMPIONS* THE ART OF THE BATTLEREALM
- *SPIDER-MAN: INTO THE SPIDER-VERSE* THE ART OF THE MOVIE
- *THE ART OF IRON MAN* THE ART OF THE MOVIE